Opening the Classroom Door

Opening the Classroom Door:
Teacher, Researcher, Learner

John Loughran and Jeff Northfield

 The Falmer Press
(A member of the Taylor & Francis Group)
London • Washington, D.C.

UK	The Falmer Press, 1 Gunpowder Square, London, EC4A 3DE
USA	The Falmer Press, Taylor & Francis Inc., 1900 Frost Road, Suite 101, Bristol, PA 19007

First published in 1996

A catalogue record for this book is available from the British Library

Library of Congress Cataloging-in-Publication Data are available on request

ISBN 0 7507 0591 4 paper

Jacket design by Caroline Archer

Typeset in 11/13pt Garamond by
Graphicraft Typesetters Ltd., Hong Kong.

Printed in Great Britain by Biddles Ltd, Guildford and King's Lynn on paper which has a specified pH value on final paper manufacture of not less than 7.5 and is therefore 'acid free'.

Every effort has been made to contact copyright holders for their permission to reprint material in this book. The publishers would be grateful to hear from any copyright holder who is not here acknowledged and will undertake to rectify any errors or omissions in future editions of this book.

Contents

Acknowledgments

We are grateful to Carol Jones for her participation and support that were important for facilitating reflection on teaching and the development of the students' perspective in this experience. The school is not named but willingly provided the opportunity for the teaching experience and continuing support throughout the study. The students in the class have new names in the study but their ideas and responses remain crucial to the story.

Foreword

There has been an increasing interest in self-study of practice in recent times. In some cases this appears to be related to the development of Schön's (1983) ideas about reflection on practice. Munby and Russell (1994) have developed these ideas to highlight the 'authority of experience' as a key to knowledge and understanding of teaching and learning. There is also a realization that there is no educational change without people change. Therefore, by focusing on personal practice and experience, teachers may undertake genuine inquiry that leads to a better understanding of the complexities of teaching and learning.

Self-study also aspires to provide a stimulus for others to better interpret their own experiences, so extending the personal benefits of self-study to new knowledge for others. Is it possible to make the results of self-study more widely available in ways that allow new meanings to be established by others? Does self-study allow for new forms of knowledge to be developed?

This book attempts to explore these questions through the experiences of Jeff Northfield during a one-year teaching allotment in a secondary school when he taught mathematics and science and was the home group teacher for one class of students in their first year of secondary school (Year 7). At the same time Jeff was the Director of Pre-service Education in the Faculty of Education at Monash University, an academic role with responsibilities and interests in teacher education, teaching and learning, and school level mathematics and science curricula. During this teaching year, Jeff maintained a daily journal of his high school activities including descriptions, reactions and interpretations associated with his teaching and his students' learning. The journal was an important part of Jeff's own self-study of his teaching experience in a secondary school.

This book is written in an attempt to find a way of informing and involving the reader in the exploration of the data gathered from the teaching and learning experiences during Jeff's return to high school teaching. It also demonstrates how the outcomes of self-study might lead to, and better inform, more formal research knowledge.

The book draws on three main data sources. Jeff's daily journal, interviews conducted by Carol Jones with twenty-two of the students in the class, and student writing from both regular classroom tasks and specific responses to classroom experiences. The journal was also read by interested teachers in the school and provided a stimulus for extended discussion about students and teaching and learning. At the end of the year, Jeff reviewed the journal and developed twenty-four theme statements grouped under five headings:

1 Nature of learning;
2 Creating conditions for learning;
3 Student perspectives on learning;
4 Process of teaching and learning;
5 Overall reactions to the experience.

Each statement summarized significant experiences and suggested possible interpretations of unresolved questions and issues related to teaching and learning. Carol spent time in Jeff's classes observing his teaching and working with and interviewing students. Her presence in the class helped her to get to know the students and to be accepted as an observer with no teaching or assessment status. Thus her interview data is most interesting and revealing. The students' writing was equally interesting as they completed specific learning tasks and other regular classroom activities.

Both of us are teacher educators trying to understand the schooling situations for which we are to prepare and support teachers. We are also searching for more effective ways to prepare teachers. It is therefore not surprising that we see the opportunity to spend an extensive period of time in school classrooms as a valuable learning experience. First-hand experience must allow a better understanding of current learning issues and should surely better inform the teacher education approaches being undertaken. The value of recent and relevant experience for teacher educators is almost regarded as self evident. However, we would now argue that the connection between school experience and improvement in teacher education is not clear. Although we would argue that greater opportunities should exist for teacher educators to work in schools and classrooms, the experience alone is not sufficient. Certain conditions for learning about teaching and teacher education need to be established to make the effort worthwhile.

In Jeff's return to classroom teaching, two conditions made the experience described in this book worthwhile. The first was the involvement of Carol Jones. Jeff needed the opportunity to interact about the student responses to his teaching and Carol helped him to do this. Carol was also able to interview students and provide a student perspective on the classroom activities and act as a colleague as the teaching and learning situations were interpreted from the perspective of all participants and their background and aspirations. The daily journal record and the variety of data gathered from the class began to make some sense. Carol therefore provided the conditions to begin learning from experience. The second condition for learning from the experience involved the first author taking an interest in the journal and the data and so continue the study. The book could not have been written without the involvement of a colleague who was able to remain at a distance from the experience and see the trends developing over the year.

The book is the story of working with a junior secondary class in mathematics, science and home group. The teacher is half-time in the secondary school while continuing to teach in a teacher education program. As well as fitting into the school program, the teacher's agenda includes looking for opportunities to encourage students to be more confident and independent learners. This concern for learning has developed from a previous teaching experience (a previous return to secondary school teaching in 1984) and a long period of involvement with groups of teachers who have developed and used teaching and learning strategies aimed at encouraging more active learning in students. These teachers provided the inspiration and ideas and Jeff was optimistic that he could make a positive contribution to students' learning and gain first-hand experience of the current issues and operations of schools and teachers. There was also a ten-week period when six of his student-teachers completed a period of school experience in the school in which he was teaching. He therefore had the opportunity to be a teacher educator working in the school as a teacher alongside his student-teachers. This provided a unique opportunity to share experiences as the student-teachers moved in and out of his class and he participated in their classes.

The major contributors to this book are the students and the staff of the school. The students' patience and willingness to express their views remain a feature of the year. Their responses to the classroom activities were very reasonable and purposeful. Schooling is an important part of growing up and Jeff's agenda for quality in learning was one of a variety of demands placed on his students. They understood his priority but it had to be accommodated as part of growing up within the classroom and school environment and Jeff felt very privileged to have been a small part of their development.

Throughout the teaching experience documented in this book, Jeff continually reflected on his teaching practice from two perspectives: a secondary school teacher and a teacher educator. He was also an experienced educational researcher and his extensive research knowledge also impacted on his understanding of this return to secondary teaching. It was therefore inevitable that he was often prompted to reflect on the nature of his developing knowledge and the implications this had for his view of research.

Richardson (1994) distinguishes between two forms of research on practice: formal research and practical inquiry. She argues that 'Both forms . . . may be conducted by the practitioner, and at times, practical inquiry may be turned into formal research . . . one could suggest, then, that practical inquiry may be foundational to formal research that will be truly useful in improving practice' (pp. 7–8). In this return to high school teaching, Jeff the researcher became Jeff the practitioner and worked from a self-study/practical research perspective through to more formal, more widely available and accessible research knowledge. This book aims to document the experiences and the resultant knowledge in an attempt to develop a wider understanding of the teaching, learning and research possibilities associated with the knowledge created and communicated through self-study.

The name of the secondary school has not been used and the students' names have been altered in the anecdotes associated with the themes. The specific experiences are presented to promote understanding and discussion of broader issues of teaching and learning. No criticism of the school or the students should be made when interpreting the anecdotes used to develop the themes. The students and the school are making very effective responses to the challenges posed for schooling. They happen to provide a useful context for considering schooling, teaching and learning in further detail and therefore increasing our understanding of these important aspects of formal education.

The book is written in three sections. The first is from the teacher's perspective whereby Jeff's journal has been used as the major data source to reconstruct some of the critical events from the year. The second section demonstrates the students' perspective and has been written using transcripts from the students' interviews with Carol, from some of their writing tasks and also using Jeff's journal. The third section outlines our thinking about the implications of Jeff's experiences for teaching and teacher education.

Section 1

A Teacher's Perspective on Teaching

The first section of this book is drawn from the journal that Jeff maintained throughout his year of teaching. At the end of each day he would devote time to reflecting on his experiences and documenting his thoughts, actions and reactions in detail in a journal. Section 1 offers an overview of the teaching year based on the descriptions in the journal. Analysis of the journal is designed to help unravel the nature of the events as they unfolded during the year and to illustrate these within the context of the ongoing struggles associated with attempting to teach in a manner that might encourage students to be more active and responsible learners.

Chapter 1

Seeking Acceptance

Overview

In this chapter Jeff's desire to add a school teaching allotment to his existing academic commitments becomes a reality. However, the level of confidence, hopes, ideas and aspirations for the venture are challenged by the reality of the daily teaching responsibilities. The classroom situation somehow limits the opportunities for the teaching ideas which were a major impetus for his return to classroom teaching and evidence of progress towards achieving his teaching and learning goals is limited. The first weeks of teaching are marked by highs and lows in students' classroom responses to his efforts.

Why Return to School

Everyone has some experience of schooling and so feels familiar with the requirements of the teaching role. The functions of teaching, and the settings in which it occurs are apparently well known. However, there are a number of reasons for suggesting that the teaching role is not widely understood. New teachers consistently comment on the difficulty in moving from the role of successful student to the unexpected demands of teaching. Public debates and media commentaries about education are based on simple stereotyped views of teaching and learning which few teachers can take seriously. Pressure groups propose that the school curriculum should include material dealing with a wide variety of social issues (drug education, nutrition, driver education, AIDS education, career education, etc.). In most cases a 'Show and Tell' approach is presented as the way of transmitting the message, despite life experiences which clearly demonstrate the limited connection between knowing about an issue and behaving in responsible ways. Most people who reflect on the impact of formal education on their lives rarely refer to the particular content they were taught. Schools and teachers have a broader agenda than the delivery of content, but there is little evidence of any appreciation or understanding of the range of purposes for schooling.

The experiences documented in this book will hopefully contribute to a wider understanding of the teachers' roles and aspirations and some of the factors which influence their students' learning. As education continues to go through changes and restructuring, often implemented by those without an understanding of the complexity of roles associated with teachers and students, it seems important to us that there be a clearer understanding of what is happening in our schools. The book therefore has, as a first purpose, the description of school activities in ways that contribute to a wider understanding of what is being attempted in our schools. There may not be total acceptance of all that is being attempted, but at least any debate should be based on a clearer understanding of what is happening. A second purpose is to prepare an account of teaching for a teacher audience. Teachers often feel undervalued, unappreciated, isolated and uncertain of their role. Some teachers (such as Carol Jones) have been prepared to describe their experiences as they tried to adjust their teaching to encourage more active learning among their students through the Project to Enhance Effective Learning (PEEL) project (Baird and Mitchell, 1986; Baird and Northfield, 1992). The PEEL project documented teachers' day-to-day struggles in helping students become more responsible learners. The effort had positive effects on their work, on their morale, and also helped in increasing understanding of classrooms for other teachers. Their descriptions of teaching and learning experiences were relevant and accessible to other teachers who identified with the issues and difficulties being discussed. It affirmed the work of teachers and provided encouragement and ideas for those who were concerned about improving their teaching and their students' learning outcomes.

The PEEL project experience has therefore encouraged us to think that descriptions of teaching and learning efforts may contribute to the professional development of other teachers. If aspects of this book stimulate discussion among teachers, in ways that some of the data and anecdotes have already promoted interest, the authors will be very satisfied. Similarly, the understanding of the complex nature of teaching and learning that is possible through such documentation should be equally beneficial to the educational research community as the themes and issues which emerge from this study are drawn from the very heart of classroom practice.

Returning to School

Having been involved in the PEEL project since its inception, Jeff clearly had a view of teaching and learning that directed his attention to analysing his own teaching practice. In his teacher education classes at university he commonly used PEEL-type activities to encourage his students to take more responsibility for their own learning and to develop their understanding in ways that lectures and other forms of transmissive teaching do not. Therefore, returning to secondary school to teach could in one sense be regarded as simply making the transition from teaching (using the same underlying principles) in one context to another. It could also offer Jeff an opportunity to pursue teaching for understanding with younger students in the very way he advocated at the tertiary level. For some, his move back into high school teaching could be seen as a challenge in which he could truly 'practice what he preached', but for others the move was less well understood.

This perceived lack of understanding by some was to be an important concern as he considered the approaching year of secondary teaching. The following extract is the first entry in his journal and outlines some of the reasons he undertook the teaching allotment.

1st January
Why is returning to school regarded as so strange (even stupid) by almost everyone. If we [teacher educators] are concerned with educating teachers and understanding teaching and learning we must have first-hand contact with schools and classrooms in a sustained way. I continue to be astounded by the number of people in the Faculty who regard schools as places to be avoided. How can we be advocates of a profession we are not willing to work alongside? How can we expect education issues to be part of policy and management decisions when we do not understand and appreciate what happens in schools? It is comfortable for many responsible for education to keep the detail of schooling at a distance — maintaining simple stereotyped views of what happens so that decisions can be easily made and justified. The closer we get to what happens in school the more we get close to people and the more difficult and complex are the decisions that have to be made.

The teaching load provides great opportunities — a Year 7 class for science, maths and home group. A lot of contact with one group of students . . .

At the same time, though, his understanding of educational research was also influencing his thinking about his return to school teaching. He was juggling the personal concerns (demonstrated above) with his ongoing professional concerns which were closely related to his involvement in, and understanding of, educational theory and research.

11th January

Bob Stake's (1992) article raises a persistent issue — the relationship between the teacher priorities in planning and understanding teaching and the objectives and approaches of course designs and text books designed to influence the classroom process. If teachers are concerned with activities and student interests and abilities, how do course guidelines and materials connect with teachers' needs? Attention is focused on the potential of the activities rather than the rationale and overall framework. The study that very few teachers understood the inquiry/ discovery concepts basic to BSCS is not surprising. Teachers were searching for other features of the materials. Without intensive inservice programs why would any teacher need to know about the underlying rationale? What are the characteristics of resources that teachers find useful? Perhaps guidelines and curriculum statements have other purposes than contributing to classroom practice?

On p. 62 Stephen Gordon (1992) describes basic paradigms explaining the way teachers are 'supervised' or treated as professionals. What are the underlying assumptions explaining the way teachers are treated? Why do traditional paradigms exist in practice where all the rhetoric argues for encouraging a more independent professional? Perhaps the way teachers have undertaken their role has contributed to conditions which limit functioning as true professionals.

Two relevant pieces of writing.

These journal extracts offer an insight into the thinking that was influential in shaping the beliefs which underpinned his view of teachers' work; perhaps not so different to that of many teachers. Jeff's concerns for both the professional life of teachers as well as how it is perceived and shaped impact on his thinking about his return to teaching. However, beyond these concerns there were also those related to his own pedagogy and how that should progress. Holding to the principles of PEEL meant that Jeff would strive to teach for understanding and encourage his students to make sense of their own learning and to be actively involved in ways which would be more demanding on the teacher than simply teaching for recall. In essence, he was hoping to teach his students in ways that involved them in their learning rather than having them attempt to digest large chunks of (sometimes seemingly irrelevant) information. Therefore, his thinking about doing this in his teaching is quite revealing when considering his upcoming return to the high school classroom.

20th January
. . . Must not set high expectations about the intensity of student thinking and learning. Gradual progress towards independence rather than burnout. Danger of trying too many ideas and gaining a stimulating but superficial response without fundamental changes and development in learning . . .

26th January
Met the class for the first time. 25 keen but nervous kids — hard to identify the problems at this stage. Really needed a couple of days to settle into the school. Still a lot of loose ends and not giving the teaching task sufficient attention at the moment. Need to find opportunities to develop ideas but conscious of trying to juggle many tasks at the moment. Perhaps I am impatient to get things underway and see what happens. The students will have to settle down before introducing new ideas. Need to develop some introductory activities for science.

29th January
Big question. How does one make a start with 'PEEL-type' activities with a new Year 7 group? The idea of going into the yard to measure a hectare did not go very well. Too long to make the measurement with too few students involved. Nothing exciting yet as we get to know each other. Need a big and satisfying activity to get us going. I am not sure it will be a planned activity. Everyone (especially me) is 'playing safe'. They are getting used to their new school and wish to feel comfortable.

So with these thoughts underpinning his initial contact with the class it is interesting to see what he recognized as important elements of learning which he linked to the nature of teaching a group of students in a secondary school.

4th February
Two reflections emerge from today's experience. Firstly, an interest in learning does not provide a useful focus in the everyday

demands of the classroom. I am genuinely trying to understand the language and thinking of students in maths but the management demands of 25 students 'swamps' everything. They appear to be coping very well but it will take a lot longer to address the learning development of kids. How does one make a classroom a place driven by learning demands? I can now see why teachers are interested in activities. Perhaps they set a situation which allows other priorities to gain some attention. Secondly, the second lesson showed how much flexibility is required. I took on board a totally different lesson from what I had planned because of what I sensed was an interest and needed to be followed up.

Everything is going well but not exciting yet — will it ever be? Am I just a person who has good ideas but will never establish the conditions to make them work in practice? I have really set myself a task. If I cannot experience some success and personal satisfaction, I have no right to interact with teachers about teaching and learning ideas. This is not easy — I need to succeed with a 'high risk' activity. They are still searching for security — the camp next week may be crucial.

It is not difficult to see how the 'return to teaching concerns' that were raised at the start of the year begin to resurface as the reality of teaching the students day by day develops. Despite the intentions associated with a PEEL-type approach to teaching, other issues inevitably influence what happens in the classroom. Teaching that is responsive to students' learning needs requires a lot of the teacher.

As Jeff started to face up to the demands of the four ten-week terms that made up the school year, this first term would prove to be crucial in shaping his view of his students and what the real challenges of teaching for understanding would entail. At the end of his second week he noted that some of the things that he thought would interest the students did not seem to 'catch on'. The students appeared to be more concerned to develop their social relationships and they worked very hard to maintain their position in the peer group.

By the end of the third week of the first term his major teaching approach revolved around lessons designed to offer students opportunities to accept responsibility for their actions. These included estimation activities in science, problem-solving tasks in mathematics and completion of a mathematics trail in the school grounds. In each case, students had to organize themselves and work at their own pace. Preparation was proving to be extensive and time consuming and he was finding it difficult to accept that this was an important limit to what could be done in the classroom. Considerable amounts of time were involved in the considerations and planning associated with the ideas for lessons and he soon recognized how much easier it would be to stick to the routine textbook presentation. Maths was particularly susceptible to the routine show, tell and practice approach. Although things were 'going OK', in his mind, it was still not yet exciting and caused him to question whether it was really possible to practice what he preached. Also, like many teachers, the realization that some feedback on his work would be both helpful and supportive was becoming apparent. He did not feel comfortable being isolated in the profession, he wanted to talk about his teaching with others, and a little feedback from the students would not go astray.

After four weeks of teaching, the limitations of the classroom (in no small part related to the constant concerns about classroom management and the influence of two or three students on the rest of the class) brought recognition of the 'low lights' of a teacher's professional life. Despite this, there was a continual struggle to shift his classroom practice to a new level supported by the ever present hope that there would soon be a breakthrough. Also, concerns from the start of the year began to return as the dailiness of teaching started to influence his understanding of his role. Even though he was an experienced and well-regarded educational researcher, and the learning from the PEEL project was an important component of that knowledge, he still wrote that, 'In the classroom, the research seems so irrelevant'. The nature of teachers' professional work was obviously more complex and difficult to understand than some research 'findings' recognized, understood, or displayed; what had happened to his own prior warnings about the clues suggested by Stake (1992) and Gordon (1992)? His efforts in the weeks until the end of term were (perhaps subconsciously) related to this matter.

22nd March
Ordinary best describes today's lesson. A hot day and we entered a science room filled with gas. So the revision sheet was completed outside. Students worked well but it is another example of contextual factors shaping what is possible even with the best planning. It is so hard to get learning onto the agenda in a consistent way. Have now reached a stage when I have many ideas but gaining the right conditions is the challenge. Also worried about some students who were falling behind.

Patrick can't apply himself and Dermot is back [a student who had been suspended due to continual disruptive behavior] but does not know how to work consistently. How does research 'factor in' the reality of classrooms? There is no doubt that understanding of context must be a high priority. My teaching goes well although the vision of developing a group of more active learners is 'fading' — but still on the agenda.

Despite the ebb and flow of these concerns the commitment to teach for understanding continued through the middle weeks of the first term. The journal writing kept returning to a theme which is often over-looked too easily by others. There is a need to be reminded how many things teachers have to keep in mind when they move in to creating opportunities for learning rather than relying solely on didactic methods. The different levels within the class are ever present with every dif-ferent task introduced. It is a full-time job responding to the range of demands and there are certainly easier ways of performing the job with much less trouble than PEEL-type teaching raises. Perhaps the important impetus to continue is related to the desire to help students develop. Seeing them learn and being a part of their development must be the tacit reward that encourages this effort. 'In the science project, Georgia, Janet and Rhonda have had the opportunity to shine and I must give them public credit for their effort. They would have been in the shadows if we were in a "Chalk and Talk" mode. Yes I do know why teachers select the riskier, messier options [for their teaching practice].'

As these insights slowly emerged throughout the term, the prob-lematic nature of teaching became more and more apparent. Lessons that were enjoyable and successful learning experiences were quickly followed by less than satisfying classes. This oscillation from one to the other highlighted for Jeff the difficulty in finding a consistent com-promise. With only two weeks of the first term remaining, he mused over an important issue in his journal.

26th March
... the following maths lesson was a struggle. Little attention and progress made and we all left very dissatisfied. It is tricky to gain the right conditions for activity and thinking and I am afraid I find it difficult to arrange and identify the conditions. They [students] expect to be activated, very few of them are self-motivated.

29th March
. . . I am sick of the call of 'Mr Northfield'. Attempts to encourage initiative and independence are having little impact with many students, they still need to be reassured — but at least they still ask for my assistance. I work hard at asking questions and building on present achievements and encouraging progress. They still respond to the immediate demands and reflection is not easy to develop. What are good strategies to begin with? Venn diagrams, asking questions? Concept maps? They have responded well to Venn diagrams but in a situation where there was a clear answer. How will they respond to a situation when there is a range of acceptable responses?

Why am I doing this? What am I learning? How much of a price am I paying as I have lost touch with the Faculty? Another period of doubt, but I have never looked backward but attempted to gain opportunities from every situation. What is the nature of the knowledge I am seeking? How will it be presented?

31st March
I am a 'product' of the sixties — to some extent my teaching style and personality sets limits on what is possible despite my views and aspirations for teaching and learning. I cannot practice what I preach — can anyone? Have thought about some ways of gathering insights about what is happening. Taking and using photos to stimulate discussion is a possibility . . .

It may be that I needed to 'live' in schools as much as returning to teaching. I have a feeling of understanding for teachers and schools. Teachers are taken for granted, everyone has experienced schools and teachers yet this wide 'knowledge' leads to a misconception and underestimation of what is involved . . .

Today — students working on their projects. Worried that I am not getting to them all but some good work being done and some confidence gained in some students. A lesson I could live with.

1st April
. . . will begin the photographs tomorrow and get the students to point the camera* and be prepared to explain why they select the 'shots'. The term is finishing up well — as good as I could have expected.

[*Note: Students were asked to take photographs which showed good learning.]

2nd April

... Forgot about the camera in the first period ... The last period had some surprises. It was an extension of the 'clothes' practical and students generally worked well. I spent time talking with individuals about their Maths project. 24 photos were taken by students as people went about their business. With 10 minutes to go Rhonda had lit a piece of material bigger than was reasonable. Smoke was in evidence and she and the class knew they had disappointed me. I expressed some annoyance and demanded a clean up immediately. Amazingly in five minutes everything was put on the tray and the benches etc. were all tidy. They had organised themselves to redeem the situation. I therefore was pleased to congratulate them and finished the lesson feeling good — and it was last period Friday. We have developed a good relationship, I have spent time with Dermot while he completes his suspension from class ... It is all worth the effort and schools can make a difference ...

As these extensive quotes demonstrate, teaching requires a genuine commitment to learning as the 'on-site' conditions within the classroom are continually changing. Teaching needs to be dynamic if it is to be responsive to the ever changing nature of the workplace. More so, teachers need to be able to cling to their hopes for their students' learning if this dynamism is to be maintained. After ten weeks of teaching it became clear to Jeff that despite his best efforts to date, that students varied in their ability to organize themselves and that it was very difficult to get to all of them. Hence class size and diversity are important issues in schooling (more important perhaps than researchers can quantify and understand despite the practical knowledge and multitude of anecdotes that teachers can supply).

On the second last day of his first term of teaching, Jeff concluded that some students were unable to work independently and that they lacked the skills and confidence to do so. This led to him to feel sad to think that their progress appeared to be dependent on the teacher always supplying work that was set out for them. Changes in class size come at a cost to individual attention and it is interesting to reflect on how much individual attention a teacher can provide, and which students actually gain attention. This makes it increasingly difficult to change students' attitudes to work and learning when the amount of time able to be spent with individuals is limited.

> *6th April*
> Dropped in to help Dermot with his project. He has run away and staff time is taken up. The 95%–5% rule again — 95% of time taken up with 5% of problem students.

This return to the concern for the individuals dominates teaching. It seems almost impossible for Jeff to feel anything but responsible for all of his students. How difficult it must be to continually balance the needs of the individual with the collective needs of the class.

In Chapter 2 we introduce the students of 7D so that the reader might begin to better understand these major participants in this experience. We consider this introduction of the students to be important at this stage as it parallels the development of Jeff's perceptions of the individuals at a similar stage in the year. Then, in Chapter 3, we resume our focus on Jeff's accounts of his teaching as we continue to see how he learns from the experience of his first term of teaching whereby he revisits and builds on many of the concerns which shaped his thinking during this first ten-week term, a term which has no doubt been crucial in his understanding of his role and his expectations of teaching and learning.

Chapter 2

Introducing the Students

Overview

The students and their responses to their formal education are essential to this book. In this chapter Jeff introduces the students through a description of a lesson. The particular lesson did not occur exactly as described but is constructed in a form that allows each of the students to be introduced in ways that represent their personalities and roles within the class. It also provides an introduction to Jeff's teaching style, an issue which will be important later in the book.

Friday: Eight Weeks into the Year

The classroom period before lunch on Friday has its own challenges. It follows a science class so we have to move rooms and line up outside the mathematics room. The science class has followed a drama session and a woodwork class so the students have been actively involved in two areas they seem to enjoy. The mathematics room is opposite the school canteen and therefore there is an opportunity for students to be first in line before the lunchtime rush — if everything goes well in the mathematics lesson. I am frequently reminded by the students that prompt dismissal is a desirable outcome of this class and my response is always to say that I will play my part, if they will cooperate.

Today the science class has gone well and we have packed up before the bell so that I am able to remind them that they will begin the problem-solving task in mathematics in the next lesson. The problem-solving tasks are a break in the normal routine and in the last mathematics lesson I had shown them the plastic boxes in which there is a mathematics problem and the associated material they would need to actively solve the problem. We had taken a box and completed a problem together and I had shown them how the boxes were labelled to show topic area and difficulty level. There is a sense of excitement about the next class as the bell rings and they move out of the room in an unusually orderly way.

I leave the class to go to the mathematics preparation room where I have selected and set out thirty boxes for the activity. The previous class is slow to leave the mathematics room so I have to wait a few minutes before moving the boxes into the room and then turning my attention to the class. They are now milling around outside the room and engaged in various ways with each other and with other students moving past to other rooms. Claire and Donna ask to go to their lockers, 'We have brought the wrong books.'

'Do we need our textbooks?' asks Rhonda, and Gary thinks that he has lost his mathematics notebook but then speculates, 'Maybe you did not give it back to me when you took it up to mark the homework on Tuesday.'

I do not respond except to raise my hands, 'Just line up quickly and quietly and we will deal with the questions later.' There is some reduction in the bubbling movement but Fred attracts my attention as he deftly uses his ruler to remove a book from the hands of a girl from 7A who is passing by. Our eyes meet and he bends to pick up the book and claims it was an accident.

'I am waiting,' is my next comment.

Those at the front of the line settle and Liz and Georgia turn and ask for quiet, 'So we can go in and get started with the mathematics problems'. A further 30 seconds and I am sufficiently satisfied to say, 'No one goes to the lockers between class periods. We do not need textbooks for this period, but you will need your notebooks. Now go in quietly.'

Some objections are ignored as the class enters the room. The entry is not good with some noise, banging of books and scrambling for desired seats. Patsy is last to enter and searches for a seat on her own while the others stand behind the tables. For an instant I consider whether I should ask them to line up again but in the end announce, 'I am waiting for quiet'. The class remains standing. Julie and Claire roll their eyes in frustration, Liz looks at me and shakes her head. Another 30 seconds and Gayle, Linda and Donna have stopped talking sufficiently for me to say, 'Sit quietly, don't touch anything and look to the front'.

Another wait before going on to introduce the activity. 'Here are the problem tasks, work in groups if you like, take one at a time and return it to the front when you are finished. In your notebooks write the name of the task, the solution and how you solved it, and whether you enjoyed the task. Now remember, we all like to leave right on the bell on Fridays, so I will be asking everyone to stop and pack up 5 minutes before the end. Any questions?'

Rhonda asks, 'What if you can't do any of them?'

'Just take an easier one and try and I will assist you when you make an effort,' I reply.

'Why do we have to write things in our books?' Jan asks.

'So that we know which ones we have done and can compare our solutions . . . Some can be solved in different ways,' I respond.

Michelle says that she does not have her book with her and Gary reminds me of his problem, 'Neither do I, it is lost,' he adds to Michelle's concern.

'I will come and see you and give you some paper when we get started,' I say in an effort to offer an easy solution and encourage them to make a start.

Linda is concerned about the purpose of the task and asks, 'Do we get marks for this? How many do we have to do?' I now realize the uncertainty a new type of activity brings to the class as I answer, 'I would rather you persisted with one problem rather than skim over 3 or 4. We might see how you go and put a problem like these on the next test'. I then motion for other hands to go down and to begin the activity. 'I will answer the other questions while you are working. Now come and select one task per group and begin working quietly. The girls in this row first.' This is followed by the usual complaints from some, 'We are always last, they will get the best ones.'

So the activity begins after about 10 minutes and the cries of 'Mr Northfield' begin.

Gary asserts, 'This is impossible.' His partner Fred is not so sure and is playing with the matches which have to be moved to make a new shape.

James and Robert have taken a box from the most difficult pile, largely avoided by the rest of the class and within minutes are writing in their books.

Liz has taken a difficult box and moved to the front of the room on her own. She is deep in concentration, shutting out the noise of the rest of the class.

Georgia and Janet have taken a box to their seat in the front of the class. Janet is frowning. She doubts that she will be successful but after 5 minutes their confidence rises and as I walk by they tell me how easy the first task was.

Patsy, as always, is working on her own. She has told me she has no friends in this class. She will cause no problems and work conscientiously but will not admit any enjoyment. School is to be endured at the moment.

Rhonda is on her own today. She expresses frustration, 'I can never do these sort of things,' she says. 'Just try,' I respond. 'What about thinking about this . . . just try and I will come back and see how you go.'

Gayle, Donna, Claire and Linda remain talking with two boxes in front of them but smile and begin to unpack the materials as I approach them. They will need to be monitored during the lesson but they are capable although rarely extend themselves.

Liz and Jan are anxious about whether they have written down their notes correctly. 'Is this what you want?' they ask. 'It is your thinking,' is my reply. Liz is not satisfied and pushes further, 'But you are the teacher, you should tell us what you want, you know the answers.' I answer again by saying, 'What you have done is fine, now try another box,' but my response does not satisfy them.

Julie, Rene and Kathy have taken an easy box and have solved the problem but want to know what else they have to do. 'It was easy, we must have done something wrong. What else do we have to do?' they say. Kathy then asks Rene to go and get another box but adds, 'But make sure it is easy.'

Patrick, Nat, John and Ken appear to have formed a coalition at the back of the room. They have two boxes with John managing the process and James acting as a consultant from time to time. Tim has his own box near this group and seems to have the ability to complete his task while participating in the mixture of work and social interaction going on.

The lesson proceeds well. The noise level is generally acceptable and the calls for 'Mr Northfield' are often to express satisfaction and excitement and show me how they had worked out the problem. One incident halts proceedings as a box and its contents crash to the floor. Gary protests loudly and blames Trish who turns around innocently claiming, 'It was an accident.'

All eyes have turned to her and she quickly realizes that no one in the room believes her. 'Well, he deserved it. He has been annoying me . . .'

I have heard enough and respond, 'I do not want to hear any more. Sit down in your seat and I will see you in a moment.'

I resume my discussions with Liz who has found a third way to solve her problem and now feels she knows what it means to understand something. 'I think there is another way,' she says, and smiles with satisfaction when I admit I had not thought of two of her solutions. I then move towards Trish, passing Michelle and Jan who both want to know if they are right while I hear Rene say, 'This is better than mathematics.'

Trish makes her case for getting even with Gary and I ask her to show me the work she has done for the lesson. As she leaves I express my wish that she not be noticed again during the lesson.

Rhonda is reluctant to make much effort and spends time attempting to link with other groups, but with little success. My hints and assistance are not followed up in a sustained way and she does not enjoy the lesson. I express satisfaction with Julie as she has completed three tasks but she is not excited and reminds me that, 'This is not real Mathematics'. For both Julie and Kathy, success has not altered their view of themselves in this subject.

I remind Gary that he seems to, 'Have done the impossible'. Peter comments, 'We are pretty good really. We just don't like to show it too much.'

As I promised, 5 minutes before the bell to end the lesson, I clap my hands and get their attention. I ask everyone to stop, check that their box contains all the materials marked on the sticker on the lid, and then return the boxes to the front desk.

There is a partial response and I increase the level of urgency by reminding them that the bell will go and that they may not be able to take up their positions at the front of the queue at the canteen. Some further activity continues then I mention the names of those who I think should hurry up.

The announcements begin to break into the classroom as the loud-speaker and the bell cause a last minute flurry of movement to return the boxes.

'We will be late. We are always late.' I ask them to sit quietly in their seats. This takes about a minute with some students urging others to, 'Sit down so we can leave'.

Silence is quickly achieved but I note three plastic boxes on desks around the room and several on the desk without lids and with their contents on the desk and the floor. My statement that, 'We will not be leaving until all the boxes are on the desk the way they were at the start of the lesson,' is met with groans and assertions that, 'They are not ours. Ours have been put back'.

I fold my arms and wait — we can hear the queue forming at the canteen. Ten seconds go by and there are suggestions about whose boxes have and have not been returned. I respond, 'I don't care, but they will be in order before we leave.' A further ten seconds pass and Gayle and Donna get to their feet followed by Georgia, Janet and Jan. The clean-up is completed in about 20 seconds and I thank the girls saying, 'I know they were not their boxes but they accepted responsibility for the class'.

The class is depressed, the canteen will now take time, the gloss has been taken from the successes of the lesson. If any gains have been made in the lesson, they have now been eroded. I ask a different row to leave first amid murmurs that, 'They always go first. It is never us'.

Patsy and Michelle ask me if I will be at the lunchtime basketball game against 7A. I had forgotten and was planning to catch up on some marking but it is nice to be asked. 'Of course, you didn't think I would miss it did you?' I respond quickly.

Trish shows me her book quickly, hoping that I will not spend any time with it. I take hold of the book and look carefully to see two problems have been noted. 'It is a pity that we have to talk about your behavior,' I say. 'Off you go.'

As she moves away she brightens up saying, 'Thanks Mr Northfield, see you at the basketball.'

I feel like she is forgiving me and I then turn my attention to Rhonda, Georgia and Janet who wish to talk about their assignments. I ask them to help me carry the boxes to the storeroom while I reassure them that what they are doing is fine and is long enough. I say again that their way of doing the problem is fine because there is no *right* way. They do not seem to be reassured.

I have no time for lunch, the canteen lines are too long and I just have time to organize the equipment for this afternoon's science class before the basketball match. My hopes for the problem-solving tasks have not been completely realized but it will be nice to interact with them in the different setting of the basketball game.

Chapter 3

Building on Experience

Overview

After ten weeks of teaching, it appears as though there is little sign of progress in students' willingness to accept responsibility for learning, and the opportunities to use the active learning strategies, which are so important in Jeff's teaching agenda, seem limited. The students are uncomfortable with the learning demands associated with his pedagogical intent and this leads him to question whether there is a sufficient level of trust within the class. He also wonders about the need for successful learning experiences to reassure the students about their ability.

Searching for a Breakthrough

With ten weeks of teaching 7D behind him, the break between the first and second terms was an opportunity to reflect on his experiences and to prepare himself for the next period of teaching. Not surprisingly, Jeff returned to the classroom still hoping to develop more responsible learners, but interestingly, looking to make a breakthrough rather than waiting for one to occur. It may well be that this was really only possible now that he was more comfortable with his position in the school, with the students and, more importantly, with himself. A period of readjustment was necessary as the change in context from teaching at university to teaching in secondary school needed to occur and be understood. At the end of his first week back in the second term he noted how his own understanding of himself as a teacher had shifted. He could see how his teaching experience was affected by his other role (teacher educator) and how that was inevitable when the researcher became the teacher.

26th April
The continued appointment with Dip. Ed. [pre-service teacher education program] means that I will not be able to ease my workload as expected . . . Still not finding it easy to develop teaching for active learning — it is easy to drop into a routine

which allows management issues to be easily dealt with. This will not be a year when my teaching will match my hopes and aspirations — I can only hope to narrow 'the gap' at times. I may be wrong but the topics don't seem to readily lend themselves to interesting teaching and learning strategies. Why am I doing this?

He had now completed a professional transition, one associated with a major shift in emphasis in the specific demands of his working environment. This is not to suggest that there was a replacement of one role with another, but that a better understanding of the routine of teaching was able to be accepted as he sought to consolidate his efforts from the first term. He begins to see limits on what is possible.

Striving for a breakthrough, and further musing over the tensions associated with teaching and research, dominated the first four weeks of the second term. The following journal extracts illustrate how these issues unfolded over time.

29th April
... The science lesson had taken a lot of thought and I chose to do the 'Lost at Sea' activity to encourage some group discussion and writing. A little disappointed with how it went yet all agreed that it was interesting and a good variation. I do feel constrained by the content of science and the gap between what I am doing and where I would like to be appears huge. I can't go on this way. Tomorrow we will try a POE as we search for a 'breakthrough' ... Our ideas about teaching and learning don't always appear to be very relevant — learning is in there somewhere.

30th April
The science class POEs [White and Gunstone (1992)] went very well because I spent more time giving some introductory notes and setting the two problems. The discussion was good and the observation for the full and empty coffee jars was clear cut. The dropping of the two jars from the tower was less clear cut. The observation that people were 'seeing what they believed' was interesting. Unfortunately the period was cut short because of a staff meeting so we could not resolve the situation ... Must think about providing some opportunities for some students to get some extra maths attention. The same students take up time in class and it is clear that some like Rhonda, Julie, Nat are less

likely to seek help. More time — there is no doubt teaching can eat up time as you try to do the right thing by all students.

6th May
Teaching reminds you of the little things, forgotten homework, forgotten books that need to be handled as you try to develop conditions and opportunities for learning.

The science class followed as we continued with the full and empty coffee jars rolling and dropped from a height. We checked our observation of the dropping jars and then discussed our explanations of our observations. Students then wrote their own responses. When I asked how many students now felt they wanted 'answers' from me I was pleased to hear the students did not feel this was appropriate. When I asked why, they readily responded that, '**We** have to understand.' 'It would not matter what you said, it is what we think that matters.' This wide rejection of the 'right answer' being provided was encouraging. They certainly saw a mismatch between the POE approach and giving a right answer. Another time when I wished I had taped the episode or there had been an outsider to discuss the student response. Within the daily routine things are happening — I wouldn't have believed it if I had not heard it.

7th May
The science lesson concluded the discussion of the coffee jars in what appeared to be a satisfactory way. The students wrote their explanations. The wet weather caused me to change plans and attempt another POE — heating a flask expanding the air and then creating a siphon when the flask cools. Very few predictions and perhaps this was one POE too many in such a short time. Less sustained interest although the task was completed and they happily wrote their explanations . . . the high points are infrequent and do not guarantee that teaching and learning will move to a new level.

10th May
. . . Do those who try to influence practice (e.g., researchers, policy makers) really understand (or remember) the practice? The theories and the 'recommendations' seem to neglect the routine and contextual complexity of the classroom setting. Many of the 'theories' seem less useful from a teaching perspective.

How do they apply to 7D on a Monday last period? Unpredict-ability is a factor — perhaps the theories come into play as I interpret the situation and respond to the way I see the situation unfolding. The best research in the world will have little impact until the conditions of teaching allow teachers time and oppor-tunities to consider ideas in relation to the classroom contexts they experience.

12th May
. . . I would have to say that most students are still very depend-ent learners and don't have the view that they are responsible for learning. Successes are few and far between and I am not able to predict when progress will be made. Can only keep trying ideas and hope to have some impact . . .

13th May
. . . I gave an introductory article on the moon and required students to create a title, sub-heading and write their reactions and questions all over the sheet. The result was reasonable — some good comments and questions which can be followed up. Very few suggested the reasons why I set this initial task — an indication that they are not used to reflecting on why certain teaching approaches are attempted and what they are being asked to do. It is now very difficult to ascertain where students are in their thinking about teaching and learning. Oh for an out-sider — am I making progress and not capitalising effectively?

14th May
. . . I must start thinking about who is responding best to at-tempts to encourage thinking/independent learning . . .

17th May
. . . following up on the moon . . . interest level remained good throughout the session so much so that we did not get to any maths activities . . . Dermot stayed involved and will try to make an effort on his own (I hope). I feel I have created a level of interest in the topic — we will see next Thursday when there will be an opportunity for those who wish to share any informa-tion to have time in the class.

20th May
I am now a firm believer that quality learning requires learner consent and really all you can do is provide conditions,

opportunities and enthusiasm. This point was driven home clearly in the science class. There was interest in the planispheres but only three accepted the offer to take them home.

24th May

. . . I can now appreciate that it takes a major focused effort for teachers to spend time interacting about teaching-learning matters. The job and time it can take up makes it unlikely that time would be available. What incentives do they have? They will go backwards before seeing any benefits. I greatly admire the PEEL effort.

26th May

. . . I am getting the feeling that they are understanding and appreciating the reasons for some of the activities. I am interested in the way many students respond to a problem solving task. When the solution is not obvious they quickly assume the inevitable failure and feel they cannot do it. Some panic and give up. The fact that <u>thinking takes time</u> is difficult for students to grasp. Success is equated with a rapid response yielding one answer — anything else is not easy to cope with. On the other hand the 'pay-off' is great when students achieve 'the impossible' as Gary did today. Yes — a good day.

These extensive extracts offer an opportunity to view the shift in Jeff's understanding of his teaching and his students' learning. A major difference between this writing and that from the first term is that he now appears to be teaching in a way that explicitly links the approach to the lessons with the learning outcomes he hopes for, and that these are connected over extended periods of time, and that the students are starting to recognize this. This change may have therefore offered the students an opportunity to view their classes as being connected rather than as single isolated lessons, a view which may have always existed in Jeff's mind but not been so readily understood by the students.

In this first half of the second term a breakthrough has been made. It may not have been some great dawning of a new age of awareness by the students, but more a gradual acceptance of what their teacher valued and expected of them through his consistent efforts to push them to better understand the purpose of the teaching strategies. Through the interaction of his thinking about how to teach for understanding and the ongoing development of his thinking about the conditions for learning with 7D, as well as the ever present concern for each

individual within the class (Dermot is a constant concern as Jeff struggles to help him, even though Dermot has learnt not to help himself)
he appears to have moved into another routine of teaching. A routine
associated with continuing to challenge the students' learning styles by
persevering with teaching strategies that do not rely on the simple
recall of factual information. This is a routine that relies on an ability to
streamline the planning of lessons so that the learning outcomes direct
the teaching approach, rather than the content being the sole source
of direction (partly noted in his feeling of being constrained by the
content of science). It appears as though this streamlining could only
have occurred through experiencing the difficulties associated with his
learning about how to link teaching strategies with learning outcomes
within the context of teaching 7D. Clearly it also required an extensive
knowledge of a variety of teaching strategies. If in this time he had
reverted to a Show and Tell approach to teaching, rather than pushing
to understand the need for linking, he could have undermined the
gains being made. In fact it may be that that is exactly what Jeff recognized himself as he struggled with his views of traditional research
(and researchers), its applicability to classroom teaching, and his
increasing respect for experienced PEEL teachers. He may have
been linking these ideas in his mind as well as in his approach to his
teaching practice.

Not unlike his students, Jeff also required feedback and a sense of
confidence and success. The nature of the workplace hinders such
feedback as professional isolation is common and the consumers of the
process (students) rarely explicitly commend or thank their teachers for
their efforts. It is largely through the implicit messages from students
that the rewards of teaching exist, but they are tacit rewards and this is
perhaps one of the difficult aspects of developing the confidence, and
maintaining the desire, necessary to sustain teachers in their efforts to
develop more responsible, active and independent learners. It is interesting to consider that if a teacher does not recognize (and respond)
to some of these signs, the window of opportunity for the learning
outcomes sought might inadvertently be closed. It must surely take a
skilful teacher to recognize the small gains and to act on them in an
appropriate way and at the appropriate time.

This period of teaching also demonstrates an interesting professional dilemma for Jeff. As he struggles with his views about research,
his statements also belie an understanding of the need for teachers
to know about, and be able to respond to, research knowledge that
is applicable to teaching and learning generally. As he continues to
push forward in the hope of helping his students to accept more

responsibility for their own learning, he considers the value in adapting what he 'knows' from research to what he is beginning to better 'know' about his group of students. Therefore he appears to be struggling with his views of research findings that claim to be generalizable. If research knowledge is to be meaningful for his teaching with his students, he needs to be able to understand it very well so that he — as the teacher — can have the necessary insights to capitalize on that knowledge. However, this requires a workplace where time to think, to share developing professional knowledge with colleagues, and to survive the disappointments of less than immediate success are constantly denied. It is little wonder that much of his writing is dotted with short state-ments questioning the value of his efforts and whether or not he is 'making any difference to his students' learning'. Yet, beyond this, his experience and understanding of research in teaching and learning still give him a reference or knowledge base to reflect on these issues, something that many experienced teachers may not have.

This continued effort to persevere with teaching that encourages students to be responsible learners, combined with 'making sense' of the context of his own class becomes more evident in his thinking mid-way through the second term.

9th June
The maths class went quite well . . . I tried to carry out the les-son (revision of geometry) by not giving an answer — shifting the responsibility to them for solving the problem and giving reasons for their answer. It worked pretty well as students con-tributed to the problems and began to realize that they knew and understood the task being set. Rhonda remained the only one who claims she can not do maths but is reluctant to even make an effort. Even she was encouraged to participate. Patrick is very weak but does try and did admit he did not understand at one point. Dermot was absent again. The new girl Fran has settled in quickly and seems to be associating with Gayle and Claire.

There is still an undercurrent of 'putting down' others which I would like to address. It is part of the noisiness that is often present, as much due to excitability as anything else. Linda, Donna and Gayle tend to be restless in the class. Perhaps they are rarely extended (Linda and Gayle especially) because they do their work effectively but in discussions they are quickly ahead of most other class members. How does one address the wide range of ability within the class? It would be easy to avoid too much discussion and opportunities to talk their way to understanding and gain confidence in public. Do we accept and adjust our teaching approach to the wide range of ability or attempt to intervene? The trouble is most interactions increase the range — 'the best get better and the worst have their perceptions reinforced'.

10th June

The double period at the end of the day proved to be most frustrating as the class was restless. For the first time I found it necessary to keep the class in to complete the tasks. Repeated interruptions caused things to move very slowly and took the gloss off some interesting achievements. For the famous scientist assignment we were able to negotiate a very reasonable set of criteria for marking the report and the oral presentation. They accepted the responsibility very well and the suggestions were very well argued. They were not prepared to assess each others' oral presentations — fearing bias in each others' ratings. I had to talk with Ken at the end of the lesson and expressed my concern at the way his behavior had deteriorated in recent weeks. Hope I made some impact. Fran is becoming prominent in the class as she tries to establish her niche in the class. Not all that impressed with some of her behavior but she may settle down. Certainly trying to establish herself in a peer group. Today it was Linda and Donna — she appears to have a similar level of ability to these two.

Certainly not a session I enjoyed — it is hard to see much evidence of progress although the negotiated criteria was a pleasant surprise. I suppose I could have 'cut my losses' and set some activities or given notes but that would have been only a management response. Balancing learning initiatives with routine activities remains a challenge. Perhaps there is not much that can be stated as generalisation. Experience, ideas and vision are all we can ask plus the conditions for teachers to learn.

Throughout this time there is the constant concern for individuals' learning as well as the learning needs of the class as a whole. It seems obvious that teaching as a profession constantly places demands on teachers' interpersonal skills as they deal with their students as individuals while still monitoring and directing the group's behavior, yet all of these skills appear to be almost subordinate to the necessary skills associated with the key role of encouraging meaningful learning. It is not unreasonable to suggest that managing the students is a full-time job on its own, how demanding must it be when learning is to be such a crucial focus?

As Jeff approached the final two weeks of the second term, his efforts to manage and understand the social behavior of his students, combined with his attempts to build on the breakthroughs from earlier in the term led him to consider, for quite some time, introducing a list of Good Learning Behaviors for his students to use as a mirror to view their approach to learning.

Whether he had realized it or not, his ability to stay on top of all of the demands of classroom teaching, and to manage them in such a way as to demonstrate to the students that there was a major purpose which directed his teaching was now an important facet of his practice. To further capitalize on the breakthroughs from earlier in the term required being able to respond appropriately to opportunities as they presented themselves. He notes how these 'intuitive' responses are more satisfying and successful (both in his pedagogy and his students' learning) and hints at what Schön (1983 and 1987) described as reflection-in-action; the practice of an experienced teacher to almost subconsciously respond to the 'teachable moment'. Yet this response is not necessarily unplanned. It may be that the moment is anticipated but the time of its occurrence is uncertain. Hence, when it does arrive, the response is almost automatic as the 'conditions for learning' are recognized and seized upon; an intuitive response. We believe that the following excerpts demonstrate this happening over time as Jeff builds on the students' reactions to activities so that he orchestrates the build-up to a 'teachable moment' such that the students believe that his introduction of the good learning behaviors was not seen as unusual, but a natural extension of their work (analysis of the students' responses to these are in Chapter 9, p. 96).

17th June
Then I asked them to share their ideas for the talk on Monday. . . . The value of checking ideas was not shared by most students — another example of the observation that students do not consider activities and learning beyond the immediate demands. To do something to contribute to next Monday was not relevant — that is next Monday . . . I asked them if they could explain their behavior. A range of responses including the suggestion that 'we are being selfish and only want to hear our own ideas' — 'we had no activities, nothing to do' — I was 'less

strict' and they were 'hyper' and tired after the earlier activities of the day.

Another disappointing day — I wonder whether I am making any progress. Indications of better learning are rare — examples of passive learning and dependent learning are common. There is no evidence that students have any inkling of why I am attempting to do certain things. Perhaps Carol can gain some insights which shed light on what is happening. If what I am doing is only perceived as 'less strict' the whole exercise is a failure. How can you give them opportunities for learning when they do not appreciate what you are trying to do? . . . I need interaction/encouragement/ideas. I feel so alone in this effort.

21st June

The talks on the scientists were well delivered and the idea of asking students to make their comments on each talk worked very well. They concentrated well for 11 presentations and the comments were very thoughtful. The written reports were well done. The students seem to enjoy doing assignment tasks like this and the two lessons went very well. Some surprisingly good efforts from a few who don't have the opportunity to achieve well (e.g., Rhonda, Kathy) . . . Just an <u>afterthought</u> — One of the features of my more successful activities with students is their spontaneity or intuitive reactions with little planning. Perhaps these are responses to students and indicate 'listening' to them. Less success with planned efforts — they are <u>my</u> agenda? Perhaps I expect too much and tend to be disappointed when the outcomes are less than expected.

24th June

. . . There is now a tendency for them to solve the tasks [activities, problem-solving exercises set for the student] very quickly. Many now have the confidence and skills to respond well and I may have to vary the demands.

25th June

. . . At some point I need to find a way of raising the issue of good learning behaviors. Patsy's talk was the last one. She always seems to be late with her assignments — perhaps she is poorly organized yet she had really prepared her talk.

28th June
Rhonda was again searching for approval but in doing so making herself less acceptable to some members of the class. Class generally worked well and then we discussed the science activity and took down the notes and results table. The science activity required carefully mixing five solutions in pairs and observing changes. They listened to and followed the instructions quite well . . . Dermot who had done nothing in both classes tipped a couple of the solutions into E to ruin the activity near the end of the lesson. Then in the final discussion Donna began putting white-out on the gas tap. This really upset the class and put him [Dermot] more 'off-side' . . . the students are happy doing the activity but are less happy explaining their results or suggesting reasons for what happened. They do not wish to seek satisfactory explanations — the experience is sufficient for them . . . I had a sense of deep disappointment amongst the class when the two misdemeanours occurred.

1st July
. . . tomorrow is a good chance to probe their views of themselves as learners . . . Linda now linked with Gayle (not Donna) and this was not a good combination today. Linda is inclined to only do what is necessary. She tends to get people into trouble at times.

2nd July
. . . I started with the reactions to the good learning behaviors. They responded very quickly to the task — it was clearly seen as a reasonable task for me to set. I was surprised at how well they did respond. There is plenty of material [for me] to think about [the students' responses to the good learning behaviors] . . .

At the halfway mark in his teaching year, Jeff has come to a point where his students appear to accept his approach to teaching and are beginning to make sense of the purpose behind it. The development towards this point has been slow and at many times difficult as he has struggled to cope with the isolation of teaching and to come to accept that, as for others, so it is for him that 'change is a process not an event'. The 'change' signs that he may have been looking for were those of immediate success, yet as he noted himself so many times, the attitudes and approaches to school that these students had developed were already the result of seven or eight years of schooling. For these students, what Jeff was working towards was now in a new context — his teaching in maths, science and home group classes — while they operated in other contexts as well. They were taught in other subjects by other teachers. Therefore, is half an academic year such a long time for the class (students and Jeff) to reach a position where they might be 'primed' to better understand and accept the challenge before them?

Chapter 4

Breaking Set

Overview

It is now clear to Jeff that the students have established expectations of schooling and have developed ways to respond to these expectations. Through his approach to teaching, Jeff is at times asking them to depart from their 'routine' and the students exhibit some concern. They quite rightly question (in various ways) the value of the new demands.

Understanding the Challenge

'Breaking set' is a term that Jeff used to describe the acceptance of the adjustments and changes he needed to make as a teacher as he learned to teach in a different context. Breaking set was part of his need to accept responsibility for what the class did and how they did it. His use of the term 'set' is similar to that of White's (1988) idea of a 'script' whereby the day-to-day events of the classroom, and the approaches to teaching and learning, follow a prescribed (or accepted) pattern. In Jeff's case, he recognized that the students had a view of classrooms, what they had to do and how they had to do it and it was one with which they were comfortable — it was generally teacher centred. Students listened, did what was necessary, and the proceedings would come to a halt at the sound of the bell. Any departure from the 'set' could lead to a favourable response if it was an enjoyable variation from the 'set', but for the students this could not become part of the set as it did not constitute real school learning; it was viewed with some suspicion. Jeff's concern was to find the right time and level of trust to introduce activities which required thinking and encouraged acceptance of responsibility for their own learning. He found it difficult when he moved from the 'set' (expected classroom approach) because of the unsettling effect created through the new situation (often accompanied by management issues). So 'breaking set' placed him in a less certain classroom environment, yet one that he was in fact seeking. As the previous two chapters demonstrate, he believed in what he was doing, but he had little recent experience at the Year 7 level, and the initial reactions of the students had worried him.

In his journal he questioned whether he was capable of breaking set as he struggled with the challenge of teaching for understanding. However, at that time, what he did not seem to recognize so readily was that breaking set was equally important for the students as it was for him. His third term of teaching demonstrated how his attempts to break set unfurled as he became more conscious of this and as the students also started to accept (and react to) the expectations of learning for the class. Breaking set was not a one way operation, the students also had to break set if they were to become comfortable in Jeff's classes.

In teacher education courses, student-teachers are commonly told that, 'Students do not admit to not understanding work, so do not ask if they understand because they will generally say yes rather than admit to needing help.' As a teacher educator, Jeff may himself have raised this issue with his student-teachers. Yet despite this, an important journal entry in the first week of the third term appears almost routine; it is entered as though there is nothing unusual about it. He notes how he feels that he has gained the trust of most of the students and that they are willing to say that they do not understand. But his immediate response to this is to link it with the management problems created as he is drawn to work with individuals rather than the whole class.

21st July
She (Jean) is an example of someone with ability — not challenged at times. I used to think the topic of multilevel teaching was an example of teachers searching for a panacea. I now realize it is a real problem. In some ways I believe I have gained the trust of most students and they are willing to say they do not understand. When they do I create a management problem as I must be willing to take up the problem yet it is of little concern to others in the class. Perhaps I need to get into the habit of small group attention while the rest of the class is working . . . I cannot connect my work to the teaching-learning strategies — my background and experiences do not allow it. Not a good time — I feel I am in limbo — not an academic or a teacher.

He considers the need to develop a habit of small group attention to alleviate this concern but does not dwell on the importance of a learning behavior that for most students is quite a change. Added to this, he is also not sure of his role.

By the end of the first week of term three he notes what to him is now a common practice. Most students complete practical class tasks quite well and accept responsibility for cleaning-up the laboratory. Through these classes he is now able to see an important difference between his hopes for students' learning, and their individual views. He recognizes that some students accept that they will not understand some areas of the work and so have no determination to fully understand everything. 'Why should they struggle and persist, not knowing something is the normal state of affairs?' His problem is that although he notes this, it is not clear that he is prepared to accept it. Herein lies the constant dilemma which causes the roller-coaster ride of emotional highs and lows as a result of his teaching efforts which so frequently crop up in his journal. He seeks to change the students' attitude towards learning. The attitude is likely to be as a result of learning to cope with a school routine that implicitly develops an attitude to learning which does not reinforce the notion of learning for understanding. The difficulty he creates for himself and the students is that he persists (just as many teachers do), but he persists beyond that which is 'normal' for many teachers. So even though the students understand his purpose and accept his view of his role as a teacher, it may be that it is in fact easier for them to accommodate this persistence rather than change to meet the real expectations. Breaking set is then an important change in behavior and doing so is difficult from either the students' or the teacher's perspective. It may well be that neither Jeff nor the students actually know what it is that they are doing as they begin to 'break set'.

26th July

Well I don't think the excitement or sense of achievement is ever going to come. Two activities designed to encourage interest and involvement were 'lost' in the continual effort to insist on attention. When given routine tasks they put their heads down and do what is required. As soon as I introduce something different requiring some thinking and activity I 'break set'. It may be a mixture of excitement and an opportunity to 'show off'. Anything different is unsettling and it would be so easy to stay with routine tasks. My admiration for PEEL teachers is immense. How did they do it? Why did they persist? The huge range of possible teaching-learning activities 'evaporates' in the reality of classrooms. Student expectations and ability to set the context are extremely powerful. The importance of encouragement and support is obvious and perhaps the effort to do it alone is too much. I wonder why I continue to search for new ideas when I am disappointed with the way they turn out . . . there is a 'dailiness' in teaching and I needed to be reminded.

As this struggle to break set persisted, or became more obvious to Jeff, learning behaviors which would have been satisfying and pleasing for him to note earlier in the year pass as routine as the changes have been gradual, and hence, not marked by revelatory episodes or events. By the end of the second week of term three his expectation is that students will complete set exercises in an orderly and responsible manner; and they do. He notes that his students have no trouble with the routine tasks, it is only when (what he describes as) thinking is required that things become uneasy. He considers trying to give students responsibilities and tasks as his experience (now) tells him that, 'they do not let you down when you put faith in them. Change of state can lead to opportunities for some active learning and thinking. Must not plan and expect too much — must remember to listen and react to opportunities. Things are going pretty well.'

As he thinks about what he needs to do to break set, he does not seem to pay sufficient attention to the same demands that the students also face to make this transition. Yet in many ways they are showing that they not only have the ability to break set but that they have (gradually) started to do so. It could be that at this time he is beginning to really see that it is for the students to decide how they will react to learning opportunities, he can not do it for them. His own insight of 20th May that, 'quality learning requires learner consent' is now lived in his own practice. His own 'living contradiction' (Whitehead, 1993[1]) may be beginning to be addressed. Perhaps this is what he notices but does not articulate in the following excerpt.

30th June

Rhonda seems to work so hard to make friends but somehow gets people offside. Some photos taken to add to our collection . . . Some good work and opportunities to help students like Patsy, Michelle etc. Not thrilled with the [externally run and administered maths competition] concept — it is designed to include items that very few can complete and therefore serves to reinforce the expectation of failure in some minds. Would not ask all to complete the test . . . Rhonda continued to be upset and Claire had decided to stop interacting with her. I have a feeling of greater confidence that I can make some progress. I don't know why — everyone seems to be fitting in (except Rhonda). Tim is on his own but does not seem to mind and he seems quite capable.

So amid the constant concern for individuals, Jeff casually introduces two important aspects of breaking set. An annual event (maths competition) which is normally administered to the students and which reinforces their normal view of classrooms causes him to downgrade its importance because of the principles that underpin it. In so doing he demonstrates that his view of the classroom and the learning he values is not the learning which the test seeks to examine. Therefore, the normal 'pressure' for all to compete and complete will not be so all pervasive in his class. He also hints at a confidence that the class is now working in a manner that is more congruent with his approach to teaching and learning, a preparedness to accept his approach more so than being so 'suspicious' of change.

During the third week of term, much of this seems to crystallize in his own mind as an important breakthrough in understanding occurs. He appears to have looked at the classroom from a different perspective, to have reframed (Schön, 1983) the problem as he reflects on a classroom episode.

2nd August
Maths class began with some discussion of the [maths] competition. Tended to be wider acceptance of the competition activities [than expected] . . . set up the demonstration of lead 'freezing' in boiling water. Not easy with the class around the front desk. Interesting to note that most people expected the lead to 'freeze' and felt that the bubbles in boiling water were steam. Some restlessness which lead me to stop everything and ask them to put their hands on their head. An interesting response was the immediate quiet. It was seen as an extreme response by me and had an immediate effect. Not a memorable teaching episode. I doubt that I am making science or maths any more relevant and exciting for students. Is it 'breaking set' for me or the students that is causing the 'problem'?

Jeff now considers an alternative view of the classroom. He has come to accept the constant struggle from his perspective in breaking set but only now really comes to empathize with the students. He believes that they must accept responsibility for their own actions, he knows that he can not learn for them, he knows that he cannot mandate their change, and now he realizes that they too struggle with the changing learning expectations of the classroom and that they have to break set if they are to move ahead in this different teaching-learning environment. After one activity in a science class when he asked the boys to role-play solids, liquids and gases, he took up a learning issue with the students. He asked whether or not they should do activities like role-plays. He believed that if he could get the students to accept responsibility for the class that they would progress further. He needed to create an opportunity that might demonstrate the value of thinking for the students.

6th August
The idea of wishing to understand does not seem to be relevant. This is not what one does at school. The maths class was an example of how quickly they will complete routine activities but when asked to show evidence of understanding, they demonstrate a resistance to thinking. Thinking appears to be something I am concerned about — not part of what is and should be done at school . . . [I need] an opportunity to do something to illustrate the usefulness of thinking . . . (Rene, Rhonda, Michelle, Gary, Fred) set limits on where you might move (the guardians of what counts as school work).

9th August
. . . this remains the main problem — extending those with the greatest ability while keeping up the confidence of some others . . . Last period was science and I introduced a concept map ['ideas map'] for change of state. After the initial uncertainties they got down to the task and seemed to understand why we were spending time on such a strange activity. It went better than I expected and I am encouraged to try the strategy again. I gave them the homework task and added a question asking them to assess their own effort and give reasons for their assessment. No surprise expressed at this requirement — perhaps this was something they expected.

It would seem then that at the very time that Jeff is questioning the need to break set (for him and for his students) that in fact that is what is slowly happening. Perhaps like many of the changes that have occurred in their classroom, the changes are more gradual than is immediately noticeable from one day to the next and that there is a lag time associated with Jeff's questioning the situation. He seems to be questioning in a way that builds on his expectations without necessarily recognizing the gains that have already been made. So it is that he considers the introduction of a long-term class project whereby the students will be responsible for a baby chick, and to measure, describe and graph its development.

As he considers the project he actually introduces the possibility to the students to see what they think about it. In essence, he checks to see whether or not they want to do the project and to formalize their responsibilities. This appears again to be an almost taken-for-granted approach to a group of students who he (at times) describes as unwilling to accept responsibility for their own learning behavior. So why does he seek their approval rather than simply tell them what they will do? The answer lies in the fact that he has come to incorporate in his practice the notion that the students will not let him down when they are given opportunities to direct their own learning behavior, and that learning requires learner consent. These assertions are now implicit in his teaching practice. Unfortunately, at the same time, as the students oscillate between their developing new set and their previous well-learned set, incidents which highlight their previous learning behavior stand out to him as more obvious than their gradual acceptance of the expectations of their new learning behaviors. No wonder he bemoans the fact that, 'They would be very satisfied if I just gave them the work to do. Efforts to have them take responsibility and think meet "resistance" . . . Teaching is comfortable until you increase the learning demands.' The corollary, though, is that learning can be comfortable too, until you increase the learning demands. Increasing the learning demands inevitably leads to discomfort; Jeff may not have yet accepted that the students have not come to accommodate this discomfort and that that is what they struggle with.

The lack of collegial contact also inhibits the articulation of this professional knowledge. It is not until midway through the third term that Jeff is reminded of the magnitude of the task he is working through.

> *17th August*
> Ian Mitchell's session in ED 4806 [Master of Education coursework subject at Monash University] reminded me of the nature of the task [I am involved in] and the time frames necessary. How did they [PEEL teachers] persist when it would have been easier to settle into 'safe' routines. The chick activity will be a turning point — I am expecting a great deal of students but wonder whether they are ready. I need reassurance that some progress is being made.

With this personal reminder he then embarked on the chick project.

A Crucial Time: The Chick Activity

18th August
Period 2 — Maths class leading to the first contact with the chickens. Everyone cooperated with a number of organizational matters. A graph plotting activity allowed me to take each of the groups to explain the use of the balance . . . we moved to room 31 to 'meet' and label the chicks. A lot of excitement and I wonder how much will be translated into useful activities. Should be an interesting opportunity for some students to display interest and involvement. Rhonda is already showing signs of creative involvement and there is no sign of reservations among any of the students. I must develop a way of assessing the way each student approaches the task over the next two weeks. **The excitement among the kids as they handled their chicks will be long remembered.**

19th August
. . . the chick activity (period 5) was particularly draining. The excitement and findings meant that there was a continuous demand for 'Mr Northfield'. Little planning at this stage but very positive efforts from Rhonda, Michelle and Fran (who do not always respond with enthusiasm). Involvement from all but I would expect quieter, better planned sessions in the next few days. A lot of care being taken with their diaries. Finished the lesson stimulated but exhausted. You need to have a commitment to a view of learning to set up teaching situations like this.

20th August
. . . Again the chick activity was high in their minds — that is really all that we were waiting for. An interesting response to the question, 'Why am I leaving the details of the chick study up to you?' There was a clear and enthusiastic response. 'You are seeing what we can do . . . You are making us responsible . . . You are seeing what we can do.' They know what I am trying to do . . . whether they accept and appreciate it is another thing. Not an exciting lesson and we were keen to get our chicks. Period 4 the activity really began. There is total involvement and the quantity and quality of work being done is amazing. Fred, Gary and Patrick seem to play aimlessly and Kathy and Julie seem to enjoy the chick — the others seem to be involved in careful study. Their keenness is evident. Moving

into quiet corners — pleading for quiet — total commitment to the task. I am not spending as much time with individual groups as I would like. A good opportunity to affirm their effort . . .

23rd August

. . . the chick activity continued but I have a feeling that some groups are playing. They are still interested and involved but they have lost a clear purpose to what they are doing. Still an excellent stimulus for writing as their diaries are extensive . . .

25th August

. . . Still a great deal of involvement with the activity and many are writing in their diary at great length. No obvious signs of boredom and two more sessions will be about the right time to finish. It is interesting to observe the way in which most cooperate.

I was amazed at the impact of the CBAM model [Hall and Hord 1987] on [University colleague] in ED 4806. In many ways it is a framework for some of my thinking. The self, task, impact concerns mirror the priorities in establishing improved learning. If self-esteem and confidence are low, little can be achieved towards completing the tasks. If the tasks are not able to be done then any reflection on learning is unlikely. The beginnings of metacognition will only occur for the proportion of students who are coping well . . . hence the tendency to spread students . . . the best are most likely to make progress. This does not deny the related effort to provide a range of activities to tap differing interests and skills.

27th August

. . . There is no doubt that they have limited ability to reflect on a task and act on the reflections. 'Preoccupation with getting the task done' seems to be the way to describe their behavior. Not unusual to have someone ask why we are doing an activity — a good sign. I wonder whether some are not being extended — thinking tasks for some are not challenging for others. I might develop a series of questions based on interpreting some graphs.

30th August

. . . the interrupted attendance of some students is a concern. Sport, Music, Roll monitors, Aerobics all cause interruptions and for some they lose the sequence of activities. No wonder there is a view that the activities are tasks to be done, not connected.

It seems clear from these journal entries that, as the students move through this extended learning activity, some of the good learning behaviors they exhibit are partially overlooked by Jeff: his 'big picture' view of his expectations of the class clouds his view of the subtle gains and changes which may be occurring through individual activities. This perhaps highlights the difficulty teachers face in trying to continuously maintain a dual perspective on the classroom where actions and events occur at both an individual and group level. Therefore, small events and episodes are easily lost or overlooked when a view of the group is so important to understanding the context of the class. However, understanding the context is one thing, being able to control it and work satisfactorily within it is another. Yet, despite all of this, important insights continue to emerge, 'It is when I depart from the straightforward activities that the challenge begins. What are the conditions which make thinking/active learning possible? I am sure they know what I am trying to do but not all are convinced that they can think or perhaps that there is any benefit in thinking.'

Jeff has reflected on his experiences in such a way as to better understand the context of this particular group of students. He has most certainly concluded that breaking set is difficult for the students and, despite his best efforts, the demands of the school environment make it difficult for the students to make the transition in learning style for which he is aiming. An important contextual feature is the peer group itself, at both an individual and class level — confidence, self-esteem and expectations are powerful shaping forces. This has been evident to Jeff for most of the year and with only a week of the third term remaining, students' responses to their own efforts continue to reinforce Jeff's view that their need for reassurance and their lack of confidence has a bearing on their learning. 'Is this all right? What does this mean? A lack of confidence in themselves and a need to be supported [is always there, just under the surface]. David [another teacher] came into the class and seemed interested in what he saw and what followed. Still [they] needed reassurance despite the fact that they could clearly understand the graphs and the 'sophisticated' questions being asked.'

The importance of the individual's view of themselves, the class as a whole, and how they fit into it was never so explicit as it became in the last week of the third term. Jeff's journal demonstrates gradual gains in students' learning behavior and his teaching approach maintains a congruence between his expectations, hopes and demands. As he recognizes and works to break set, and as the students seem to be struggling with the same problem from their own perspective, the two collide in an unexpected and unforeseen manner.

10th September (Friday)
Period 3 was excellent with the students setting up their circuits and showing the compass moving under the copper wire carrying the current. Good tidying up and everyone was pleased with the effort. Period 4 — what a contrast. Began with Linda giggling and Trish following. Return of the test interrupted repeatedly and distribution of the maths project became difficult. Moved from warnings to keeping them in to stopping discussion queries on the test. Questions on the project then followed with Fran immediately asking Jan's question after it had been answered. Not a pleasant lesson — all were kept in and then Linda, Gayle, Trish, Fran and Rhonda stayed on. A strange discussion. What was originally presented as a giggling episode extended into a feeling that they were sick of being treated as the good class of 7D and needed to rebel a bit. They did not want to be regarded as 'good students'. They will sit as far apart as possible and agreed that they were selfish and poorly behaved. They pointed out that they had not been this bad before. Rhonda and Trish were the least mature of the five. We will see how things go in the future. My anger and disappointment were clear — I hope.

11th September (Saturday)
Some reflections: . . . Can I ever compete with the powerful effect of peer group responses outlined yesterday. These students felt they couldn't continue to be doing well. As I review progress to date, Rhonda, Linda, Fran and Trish are certainly not responding well. Rene and Patrick are not making progress. Where do we go? A more 'aggressive' use of active learning strategies? What has been achieved?

These two journal entries are significant. As Jeff reflects on the nature of the peer group and his role in encouraging the students to be active and responsible learners, he is confronted by a puzzling (and worrying) situation. Some of the students are choosing not to accept the opportunities for learning being placed before them. More so, they are adopting behaviors that will also make it difficult for other members of the class to benefit from the learning opportunities as they purposely disrupt the lesson. His observation (6th August) that some members of the class felt a need to be the 'guardians of what counts as school work' is certainly being realized now. It is little wonder he struggles to feel as though he is making a difference to his students' learning. There is always something looming in the background to divert his attention.

13th September

The struggle continues. The group of girls causes concern and persist in creating an unsettling influence. (Linda, Fran, Claire are unsettling a few others and beginning to annoy others in the class). The maths class was devoted to beginning the project. Most students were busy very quickly, mainly on survey questions. Questions for a trivia quiz were developed to be presented later in the double period. A lot of questions, some [students] still needing affirmation but in general the lesson went well. In the next lesson the questions about the nature of electric current were presented. Then the small unsettling actions began to occur. The review of the questionnaire was interrupted — Fran was asked to stand up and the last row of the girls were asked to remain behind again. Are they achieving their aim to be more rebellious. In the next lesson I will give them the option of being part of the lesson and try to isolate them if they do not participate. The other members of the class are becoming as annoyed as I am. Management is no problem, but effective learning conditions are becoming harder to achieve . . . It remains a fact that setting routine tasks will lead to no problems. It is when discussion of ideas is attempted that the class is exposed to unsettling responses. Girls attempting to establish their status among their peers. Where are my teaching-learning theories now?

This struggle with the girls who have decided to react to the learning demands of the class is an important episode. In many ways they demonstrate that they have realized that they do have some control over their learning environment and that they can actively shape it in ways which they prefer. Although their behavior is unacceptable in light of the learning approaches being sought, their response demonstrates that their confidence is tied to a view of themselves. A view that has already been shaped through many years of schooling. They lose confidence when they attempt to learn in ways which are counter to their view of themselves and their ability. The third term ends with a most apt reminder of who these students are and how they view themselves. An important factor in shaping their understanding of what comprises school teaching and learning.

> *15th September*
>
> Home group — a video *Beauty and the Beast* — I am reminded that they are really 11–12-year-olds searching for their identity and not always growing up comfortably . . . They very much respond to the immediate task and the moment. They don't seem to accept the possibility of controlling their situation. This partly explains their continued dependence and need for progress to be affirmed. Independent learning is therefore going to be beyond them until they have the confidence and ability to see that they create their own situations to a large extent. Learning is something that happens to them not something they feel they can have control over.

Through this extract, which closes his third term of teaching, Jeff appears to be reminding himself of both the task at hand, in terms of his hopes for his students' learning and his teaching, and the demands that this places on a group of students who really are still quite young and immature: students who are still forming a view of themselves and how they 'fit in' in a complex and demanding world.

Note

1   Whitehead (1993) describes a 'living contradiction' as the recognition that one's educational values are not truly being lived through the educational practice employed. In this case, Jeff's valuing of students' need and ability to make their own choices is challenged by his desire to have them make (what to him is) the 'correct' decision about how to approach learning.

Chapter 5

Maintaining the Effort

Overview

After three terms of teaching there are signs of student progress in their approach to learning. The students are becoming more comfortable with demands which encourage acceptance of a greater responsibility for learning. This may not necessarily indicate a commitment to more active learning but it certainly suggests that there is an acceptance of what Jeff is trying to do.

Is there a Sense of Progress?

The fourth and final term of teaching 7D would be characterized by an attempt to diminish the gap between Jeff's expectations for his students' learning and their own expectations of what this should involve. At the same time he would continue the ongoing struggle to try to re-shape his students' views of themselves (more important in some cases than others) so that they might become more confident in their ability to learn. Even though the year was coming to an end, Jeff was still searching to create opportunities for his students to accept more responsibility for their learning. His ability to persevere would continually be tested as the distraction created by some would lead to a restlessness that needed to be monitored.

In science at the end of the first week he introduced a lesson on the Discovery of Velcro. The students knew the purpose behind the activity, 'to make us think and understand', and the creative thinking aspects of the activity were acknowledged but not valued, largely because four students' behavior shaped the lesson. The lesson was therefore viewed by students more as a task than as a learning activity and Fran and Michelle were two who had a profound influence in this respect.

For the next two weeks this led Jeff through a cycle of thinking in which he questioned his students' desire to understand. His observations showed that, for some, determination to understand was something rare. Further, acceptance of the inevitability of not under-standing seemed like it had been etched into their minds. Because of these observations and thoughts he struggled to convey a feeling of what it 'means to understand' despite believing that some of his students did not 'expect' to understand. The issue was exacerbated by the fact that the students' image of the purpose of school was very powerful and did not fit with understanding as an outcome of learning.

Maintaining a clear purpose for Jeff's approach to teaching seems to have been an important shaping factor in his impact on the class. He persisted by offering independent learning opportunities, despite the concurrent management problems they tended to create, and there was some recognition of the effects among the students.

> *16th October*
> There has been a change in the last week or so. I am tending to set work and expecting them to make more attempts to organize the priorities, and it seems to be working. Perhaps we are demonstrating mutual trust. This will certainly continue this week if I am to require demonstration of understanding to redeem maths marks and student opportunities to complete their science projects. Is this a permanent development or a lull? Do I have the nerve and confidence to give this a real chance? It does allow me to get to individuals who seem ready to be encouraged and supported.

One of the most disconcerting aspects of his perseverance (which must surely have had a dampening influence on his recognition of the gains made) was that the better students tended to accept and learn from the opportunities he created, while some others did not want to accept these opportunities as they did not want to take the risk of further disappointment: this would only serve to reinforce their existing view of their ability. 'This approach is a partial success and I will persist . . . the trick is to have activities which keep them involved and allow me to spend time with individuals and groups. I will never get all people involved but I think they are beginning to see what I am trying to do.'

An important change in the nature of the class was precipitated when the group of girls who had been a disruptive influence to the rest of the class were subject to interim reports. This school level response to their behavior caused them to be much more careful and allowed the class to operate better as they began to organize themselves and coop-erate. This decrease in management problems was most evident and pleasing for Jeff.

22nd October
A big change today. The group of girls have been the subject
of interim reports . . . A satisfying lesson with students at different stages yet little or no management issues to upset the flow
of activity. In the maths lesson I introduced the idea of doing
an example at the front when they believe they understand the
idea in the set of activities. It was well accepted by the kids. The
hope is that it will encourage them to ask the question about
understanding and make a decision about when they think they
understand rather than just completing the problems that are
set. An element of mastery also as they will take different amounts
of time before they feel they are ready — an element of confidence involved . . . I needed to have a good day after a hard
week.

27th October
It is worthwhile (today). Home group is an interesting opportunity. I am not a maths teacher or a science teacher — perhaps
just a person. Moving around to sign their diaries Fran and
Gayle and Michelle were talking about school and teachers.
They said I was patient and they knew what I was trying to do
but they knew they did not always respond well. The peaks
and troughs I have are my reactions and are not the way the
kids see it. They bear no grudges, each lesson is a new event
and they do not like to feel teachers are picking on them . . . the
maths lesson went quite well. Some of the better students have
the confidence to tackle the task.* The weaker students are still
hesitant. They lack the confidence and why should they risk
failure by coming out to do the task . . . they were willing to
organize themselves and work independently. The weaker students now become a concern. (*See 22nd October)

Also, as the constant concern to help students develop their understanding persisted, breakthroughs occurred at the most unexpected times
and amidst unusual contexts.

29th October
. . . The 'critical mass' to take the edge off a lesson or activity is
quite small. Three or four opting out can reduce effectiveness
especially when they distract others. So we again faced the
complexity of context and daily variations in students and the
opportunities were not successfully used . . . Consider Fran.

Midway through the lesson she expresses no interest in electricity, 'It is boring, I don't understand anything.' She goes to the circuit boards and successfully sets up the circuit which addresses the problem. She is excited. She admits she doesn't know why she did not try, it is interesting and she has a good sense of achievement. Perhaps there is [only] so much energy that can be invested in the school day and we expect efforts throughout the day.

Individual recognition of breakthroughs such as this occur throughout the journal, and many have been reported here, but from Jeff's perspective there is not a continual sense of personal satisfaction with the cumulative effect of these achievements. Therefore, in this last term it is interesting to note a mild sense of satisfaction creep into his writing when, for an extended period of time, he focuses less on the peaks and troughs associated with his teaching but more on the outcomes themselves. Perhaps this was partly a response to having Carol (Jones) in the class, combined with a recognition of some of the opportunities for learning that the students accepted, mixed with an understanding of his reflection that, 'there is only so much energy that can be invested in a school day'; an important point to remember.

In early November he notes with satisfaction that some of the students who had worried him with their lack of involvement and application had completed their tasks. He writes about the opportunities for organization and independent work within the classroom with some certainty and confidence, '. . . most students are working well . . . a lot of activities are now falling into place . . . I should be in a position to assess those that have made progress in the next few weeks. I feel quite good today.' This is in fact quite high praise in Jeff's writing as he more often than not focuses on the difficulties created through success rather than the success itself. The following excerpts demonstrate this point, and perhaps at the same time encapsulate the dilemma of teaching.

4th November
Another reminder of the amount of organization and time needed to prepare for today's class. Period 4 Science — fake skin/wounds, Period 5 groups on different tasks — video, repeating test items, problem-solving tasks. It is both organization and management that sets limits on what can be achieved when you try to individualize. I felt exhausted by the end of the day. The wounds session went very well and students appreciated the

activity. There was too little time but there was a sense of success. Carol was involved and then interviewed Linda and Gayle. Maths — the video film was repeated and the points about understanding of ideas was made as I outlined some problems appearing on the maths test. The peer pressure to behave reasonably is now very obvious and waiting for silence is now immediately associated with demands from students [for quiet]. Suddenly there is plenty to do. I wish I could make some progress with the slower students. They are the ones who suffer most with the constraints of time.

6th November
It is easy to be disappointed but some of the students completed very thoughtful concept maps. Many are not prepared to spend time in something that does not have a clear answer. There is little concept that they make their own knowledge and understanding. They see schooling as gaining knowledge by transmission in a passive way. Nothing I can do can change this perception in the short term. It is so disheartening but any efforts on my part make the situation worse for many students. Why should they move away from the known and certain?

10th November
Rhonda gave up — again — but by the end of the lesson she was asking for work. Her efforts are so spasmodic. I am not sure she has ever experienced a consistent effort resulting in progress. Very active involvement by Gayle and Linda. They have a great deal of ability and energy when they harness it in a positive way. I feel that 7D are in a pattern of work which is acknowledging their ability to organize themselves and accept responsibility. Most are doing this most of the time. However, what will tomorrow bring?

Reflecting on the Experiences with the Class

An important contextual factor which appears to have quietly become part of the working of the class is trust. Jeff mentions it at different times and in different ways as he reflects on the importance of *confidence* and *responsibility*. The development of both of these seem to us to be crucial elements of trust. Trust comprises a number of forms similar to those so well documented through the PEEL project (Baird and Northfield, 1992, p. 92). There is a student trust that the teacher will show interest and support for ideas, and a trust that the teacher will control, direct and respond to questions appropriately. There is also a trust that students will be supportive of one another and a trust that confusion created through learning will be resolved. However, trust is not quite as straightforward as recognizing these four conditions. In this class, trust is a reciprocal event. Jeff needs to be able to trust the students and they need to be able to trust him, which is much more than simply acknowledging the need for these conditions. The trusts need to be 'lived' through the teaching and learning if the risk-taking associated with breaking set and accepting the challenges offered through such opportunities are to be grasped.

In mid-November Jeff notices this himself as he recognizes that the theme of trust appears to be seen as important in the class. The ability to build this sense of trust must in some way also be related to the amount of time that they all spend together. As their science, maths and home group teacher, Jeff has a lot of contact with 7D. Perhaps it is this point, or the fact that the peaks and troughs have (to some extent) levelled out, that causes him to return to the educational literature — or link his reading to his current position — so that he recognizes the unique position he is in.

23rd November

I suspect I am missing 'signals' and opportunities. This is what good teaching is at this level, being sensitive to the signals — linking your agenda to their readiness. However, the group is not homogeneous . . . as soon as you make progress with one or two, other demands emerge. It is like trying to hold onto jelly — you simply engage in the struggle you never achieve progress overall. Teachers who only have the class for one subject and perhaps only one semester must never 'wrestle' with the individual development issues. Perhaps it is just as well but teaching must tend to become an issue of delivery . . . Beginning to look to the literature to assist interpretation of my experiences. The literature seems clear and ordered when compared to the 'messiness of the swamp'. Generalizations don't seem to apply among the day-to-day variations of the class. The reservations about the same teacher for maths and science may indicate doubts about accepting responsibility for their behavior. Easier to start again, each lesson a separate unit is a way of coping. Making connections means accepting responsibility.

The 'messiness of the swamp' may appear to be an apt way of describing the complex nature of teaching and learning in schools, but it is also simplistic to consider it as a 'swamp'.[1] The swamp is really more an array of interconnected sets of events, personalities, social and intellectual abilities, individuals and groups, all of which are seen differently depending on the time and perspective of viewing. So to the casual observer it may appear to be a swamp, but to the skilled pedagogue it is a kaleidoscope from which different possibilities emerge. An example of how Jeff as a skilled pedagogue is able to work in, and shape, the swamp is evident in the trust that he has developed as a crucial element of the classroom environment. It has become a part of the fabric which holds his swamp together and allows it to be charted.

In the last week of November he asked the students to construct their own 'personal report' on their progress in maths and science (see Chapter 10 for examples of these). They performed the task and demonstrated again that they were used to Jeff's 'unusual requests', there was a sense of trust and of understanding the purpose for the task; something which was only possible if the swamp could successfully be navigated. Considering the fact that at this time Jeff had also come to the conclusion that there was a widespread feeling that understanding should happen without any effort on the part of the students, and that he believed that all of the students wanted to do well but did not want to be a member of the class that does well (they wished to be 'cool', not smart), this personal report task could easily have been interpreted as going a little too much against the grain.

It could well be that on reflection this same idea was triggered in Jeff's mind for at the end of November, as he mused over his expectations of the students and compared them to the students' own expectations, he started to consider offering them the opportunity to construct their own report on him. In many ways this could be seen as a leap of faith, but in others it is more an indication that teaching and learning in 7D was a joint responsibility; either way, it would only be possible in an environment where trust was a two-way process. While all this was occurring, Jeff was reminded again that he was still working with young students, yet his expectations of what was reasonable and responsible did not align with more common community views of the expectations of 12-year old children.

1st December
. . . maths allowed us to make a map of the time capsule and
then a game of 'Foxes and Hounds' down the back [of the

room]. They are really still children in many ways and I wondered how much I should be expecting from them. The social and context[ual] factors that set limits on their 'active' learning seem obvious and reasonable now. Perhaps interventions need to be directed towards improving social skills, building self-esteem, rather than the teaching-learning strategies which they may not understand or are incapable of doing effectively. Trish indicated that she would miss me next year and seemed to mean it . . . they seemed to be quite happy that I asked them to write a report on me. Perhaps they do trust me — or they don't question a teacher's request. A pleasant morning . . .

This shared responsibility within the classroom was also highlighted by Jeff's approach to the students' end of semester reports. He wrote — almost as if it was common practice amongst teachers — that he would give the students their grades and talk to each student individually about their progress. This approach reflects the sense of trust that Jeff had created in 7D, he had to write a report on each of them and he wanted to discuss what he had written and why with each student so that they better understood Jeff's view of their achievements. Also, discussing the report in this way could be quite a risky exercise so recognizing the implicit message Jeff was giving the students in asking them to write a report on him is important. This was a classroom with shared responsibilities. If the students were to understand what it meant to write and discuss a report, they needed to also experience doing it.

8th December
A good day although I was apprehensive about what might happen. Their report about me was well received with some reluctance on the part of a few . . . Took them outside for the last period. They seemed to agree with the grades and there was some good discussion about the individual comments I made to them. Trish, Claire and Linda were very interested and good discussion followed. Nat and Ken were very pleased to have the talk and most appreciated the opportunity to be treated as an individual person. I like them all as individuals although in groups at times I am less enthusiastic. The year has not been all that I hoped in some ways, yet it has been better than I had hoped for in others. Look forward to reading their reports on me. Will miss the teaching but not the situations and conditions in which teachers find themselves.

This journal entry demonstrates how the students had learnt to accept and respond to the opportunities for learning, cooperation and responsibility which Jeff had offered them throughout the year. The two approaches to report writing could have a number of student reactions (not all favorable and is no doubt why Jeff was a little apprehensive) yet, as he had come to know, when the learning tasks were appropriate and reasonable, the students were more than capable of accepting responsibility for their actions; they did not let him down.

With the end of the teaching year upon him, Jeff finally gave himself a chance to reflect on his experiences in a manner which allowed him to see something more than just the complex but discrete units of individual lessons and days which, in many ways, directed his thinking throughout the year. With the formal end of school culminating in Speech Night, he concisely summarized his understanding of his view of school.

14th December
Speech Night: Another satisfying event to end the year. The school has a great deal to present to the community. Music and sport are big contributors. 7D was well represented in awards. 16/25 received awards with James dux. For some there was a struggle (Gayle, Linda, Fran, Ken, Michelle) but clearly the effort was worthwhile. Most people had developed during the year and can look forward to the future in schools.

It is interesting to consider how much of his confidence in his students' development could be attributed to the effort he had made throughout the year. He did not feel that he had created a class of 'super, responsible, active learners', but he had certainly had a major impact on their approach to learning and their expectations of themselves. In Section 2, we explore this from the students' perspective.

Note

1   The swamp metaphor prompted one teacher colleague to write, '. . . don't forget the swamp is a wonderfully rich and diverse biosystem. Lots happening, lots growing, but only very slowly evolving. Maybe that was 7D.'

The Students' Perspective on Teaching and Learning

Section 2 moves the focus on the teaching and learning in the classroom from the teacher to the students. This section is drawn from the insights gained as a result of the involvement of Carol Jones with both Jeff and the students. Throughout this section, the students' understanding of their experiences within the classroom is highlighted and demonstrates how important their perspective is when attempting to understand the dynamic nature of teaching and learning.

Chapter 6

Different Versions of the Same Experience

Overview

To introduce this section of the book one lesson is highlighted to develop the tensions between Jeff's agenda and the students' ways of coping with their schooling experiences. The students appear to be aware of the teacher's purposes for the activity but are unable to accept the validity of the task. This chapter uses a classroom episode to begin to present schooling from the students' perspective.

Outcomes and Matching Intentions

The teaching and learning experiences in Section 1 have been documented from Jeff's perspective as the teacher. In order to enhance the view of the classroom we now offer the students' perspective. We start with the Velcro story because it provides an example of the types of learning activities which were introduced to encourage thinking among students.

In Chapter 5 we briefly mentioned the Velcro Lesson (7th October). Such active learning tasks met with mixed success and later sections will attempt to interpret these uneven and unpredictable responses from students. However, one of the reasons why Jeff undertook the teaching allotment was to seek opportunities to use these type of activities; as other teachers had shown the positive impact they had on students' confidence and ability as learners. The lesson is also the time when Carol appears in the classroom and begins her first interactions with students. They begin to learn who she is and the role she will play in listening to their perspectives on teaching, learning and schooling. Carol's arrival initially led the students into a position whereby they had to come to terms with a new person in their room. This could also be seen as a major agenda item which encouraged competition within the lesson activity.

The account of the lesson introduces the importance of the context in which teaching and learning occurs. At first glance much of this context remains obscure, although experienced teachers seem to be aware of, and intuitively respond to, these background factors as they take them into account in their teaching. Carol is to provide a way of making this context more visible as she interacts with students to clarify how they are thinking and the ways they perceive schooling. What happens in a classroom is more clearly understood as we know more about the wider context. We can then understand why the group of four feel the need to change the class image. We can see why the students seek to make class lessons separate events so that each lesson allows a fresh start. These are the background factors so crucial to understanding students' responses to classroom events. These form the contribution which this book attempts to make towards understanding teaching and learning a little better; a contribution from the students' side of the desk.

The Lesson: 'The Story of Velcro'

> Well if he does boring stuff like Velcro. You don't really want to learn about Velcro. . . . Besides, when you're old it's not as if someone's going to ask you, 'Do you know where Velcro comes from?' (Donna)

The 'Velcro lesson' captures some of Jeff's hopes and aspirations for the teaching experience. The task for students was to read a short account of the discovery of Velcro. The title and sub-headings used in the original story were deleted and students were first asked to write in appropriate sub-headings and provide a title for the story. The activity represented an attempt to give opportunities for students to be more active in their learning. Past experience had suggested that these tasks, in association with the reading, encouraged a more careful and thoughtful response to the story. The description of this lesson is therefore chosen because it indicates the types of thinking activities Jeff was seeking to introduce. It also allows us to introduce the student responses and tensions that often emerged in the classroom.

The Velcro lesson was the first time that Carol met the class. She was introduced as a person who would visit the class regularly and talk to students. Her presence caused an atypical response as they all (teacher and students) began to come to terms with another participant in the classroom.

This account begins with an extract from the journal. The extract extends to comments about the following lesson on that day and an extract from the following day to place the Velcro experience into a wider context and show the short-term nature of the student responses. Each lesson is, to some extent, a separate event for the students.

7th October

What a day. Carol came to the first lesson and they were restless. The group (Linda, Gayle, Fran and Claire) were keen to establish their status. The Discovery of Velcro — was done as a routine task. They knew what we were trying to do, 'make us think and understand'. The creative thinking aspects appeared to be acknowledged but not valued. The group took most of the 'air-time' making responses and looking for approval. In fact they are gaining little support from their classmates (except Trish and Rhonda at times). Carol seemed to get good responses from Michelle and Fran but in fact they (the group) are gaining too much of the time and others are being left. Good discussion with Carol afterwards and she seemed to be more accepting of the situation and did not regard it as a lack of progress. When (if ever) do students value thinking? An unsatisfactory lesson although only 4 out of 25 shaped the lesson. The final discussion was disappointing for this reason. The lesson after lunch was remarkably different. The group (now separated to some extent) made an effort. The small amount of work did not extend some but there was an opportunity to help a number of people. My worries about the behavior in the class brought a response from Gary ('Kick Fran out') but my dissatisfaction is known and some response is evident.

8th October

A good day. Dean [a student-teacher] came to take them for maths project tasks for the two periods. Fran and Gayle asked for the opportunity to work with Linda in a group and assured me that they would prove they could work together. By the end of the double lesson I was able to congratulate them on working well. They had proved me wrong. Much of teaching is creating the conditions where learning might occur. All students were involved in the activities and good work was done as they wrote up one activity. Great improvement with Michelle and continuing improvement with Rhonda. They enjoyed Dean's teaching and his presence gave me the opportunity to get to a number of students and provide encouragement. Also an important opportunity to talk with students in other than a formal teaching role. They are quite good at solving the problems and their confidence increases with these tasks.

The Velcro lesson was a disappointment if one considers the purposes for the task. 'They knew what we were trying to do', but there were doubts about whether this was a valid task in the classroom. 'Why should we write a title when it is probably going to be wrong?' 'Who wants to know about Velcro?' The activity can be seen in the wider context of a small group of four students who were uncomfortable because, at this time they were being labelled by friends in other classes as members of 'the best Year 7 class' — a statement being made by some teachers. This was not an image they wished to retain and they were seeking to make themselves and the class more 'normal' (see Chapter 7, The Goody Goody Class, p. 72).

Carol's Perspective on the Lesson

Carol's presence created a new situation for the students to deal with, and the lesson was inevitably a time of re-adjustment for the class. Carol's initial reactions to the class add to the story of the Velcro lesson.

> It was my first visit. Jeff and I arrive at 7D's assembly point to watch 7D straggle into place in 'dribs and drabs'. Each group announces its arrival boisterously.
>
> 'Hi Miss!' one of the girls says cheerily at the top of her voice. 'What's your name?'
>
> I try to look friendly but innocuous when I answer (I don't want to appear too familiar too soon but neither do I want to assume a teacher role). 'I'm Miss Jones. What's your name?', I asked.
>
> 'I'm Fran!'
>
> 'I'm Michelle!' shouts another.
>
> 'I'm Linda and this is Gayle!' The girls call out names and vital pieces of information about themselves. I wonder whether they are always this restless or whether they're keen to impress the visitor with their charm! The boys are noticeably quieter but jostle each other good naturedly.
>
> Once inside the science room the noise level increases. A group of girls immediately and loudly take possession of the back row. My new acquaintances, Fran and Michelle, are there.

Other girls fill the next row while the boys arrange themselves at the front. Jeff tells me later that this is the opposite to the usual arrangement. One of the girls is having trouble finding a seat. She is invited to join two groups but distances herself deliberately by moving a chair to a vacant bench in the third row.

Jeff tries to start the class several times without much success. The back-seat girls call out interruptions and squirm around while the front-seat boys are more quietly subversive. As one trouble spot is smoothed over another outbreak occurs somewhere else in the room. Eventually Jeff waits in silence (and waits and waits) and after some time the lesson begins.

Over coffee in the staffroom 'The Story of Velcro' had seemed like a good idea. A neatly packaged, self-contained lesson, just what the teacher ordered. Read an interesting scientific anecdote, interact meaningfully and personally with the text by making up your own heading, looking for unfamiliar words and designing your own questions; then participate in a stimulating class discussion leading perhaps to a well-taken point about the serendipity of scientific discovery. Voila!

That was the plan anyway.

Why then did Linda spend the entire lesson coloring in her science book with a lurid silver marker? Was it really necessary for Rhonda to ask every girl in the class if they knew what to do and still not start the task? Did Fran and Michelle need to spend quite so long discussing what they planned for the weekend at five decibels? Does the quest for a red biro always turn into a wrestling match amongst 13-year-old boys? And why was a quarter of the class out of their seats at any one time?

I circulate, chatting to students. Fran and Michelle volunteer that they aren't interested in the story of Velcro. 'It's boring! What's it got to do with us anyway?' They like 'doing things', subjects like physical education, drama and art, rather than 'thinking about things'. History is also considered irrelevant although it sometimes has a bit of relevance they concede if it is about something current they are interested in — like the Olympics.

I ask them what they would find interesting in science and they can not think of much. Michelle says blithely that it isn't necessary to know how or why things work, only to be able to use them. Fran thinks that evolution and creation might be interesting. Even so, they tell me that Jeff has to make them do this stuff because, 'It's his job'. That doesn't mean they have to show any interest in it.

Amidst the disruption most students tackle the work and a short discussion ensues but it is marred by constant interruption. Quite a few students have their hands up at various times but aren't asked for their contributions as Jeff is dealing with miscreants. Some appear annoyed.

The discussion jerks along to a conclusion just before the bell (could students have cooperated just enough to get out on the bell?) and perhaps surprisingly many students come to the point about scientific discovery which Jeff was hoping for. Most have completed the set tasks.

I leave feeling that I have just met a fairly typical Year 7 class, one which is reminiscent of many I have encountered before [in my own teaching].

The Students' Perspective

During the following ten weeks as Carol interviewed class members, ten students raised 'The Story of Velcro' spontaneously. John and Nat merely mentioned it and laughed; one wonders why. Most of the ten mentioned it in the context of boredom and several then proceeded, like Donna at the beginning of the story, to wonder at its relevance.

Carol:	When you do something in science can you usually see why Mr Northfield might want you to be doing it, learning it?
Georgia:	Oh, sometimes.
Liz:	Sometimes. But with the Velcro, I don't know. I don't see. I suppose we kind of did it . . . I don't know. Why'd we do the Velcro?
Georgia:	I don't know.

So despite all the good intentions of the teacher, despite the planning, thinking, organization and (hoped for) relevance, a good idea for a thought-provoking lesson designed to encourage students to be actively involved in their own learning does not appear to have lived up to expectations. But this is an important aspect of the nature of teaching, learning and schooling, so the story of Velcro offers an appropriate focus from which to begin to explore these further. It will be referred to to illustrate later ideas and allow comparison with other classroom experiences. The Velcro story demonstrates well how all of the concerns and issues that dominated Jeff's first term of teaching continued to re-surface and interact throughout his teaching. For Jeff as the teacher, being concerned with individuals, with the class as a group, and with his own desire to develop more responsible learners, required a deeper understanding of the context of learning with this particular group of students; and it may well be that such an understanding was only possible by researching his own practice. In the next chapter, 'A Focus on the Learner', we introduce some interrelated assertions about learning which seem to us to be a useful framework to interpret students' responses to a number of classroom situations. We also present the way the students see schooling; they are constructing their own understanding and then behaving according to their perceptions.

Chapter 7

A Focus on the Learner

Overview

By exploring students' views of schooling a complex array of factors begin to be uncovered which start to explain the diversity of individual responses in the classroom. Each student is developing a self-image and classroom experiences that are both affected, and shaped, by their past and contemporary experiences. As one begins to know about the lives of young people, some understanding of their classroom responses emerges.

A Failure in School

After seven years of formal schooling these students have developed views of themselves as learners and the role schooling occupies in their lives. These personal views must therefore inevitably influence their learning behaviors and their responses to Jeff's teaching approaches as he forged ahead with his desire to develop more active, independent and responsible learners. At the same time, they are developing powerful views about their schooling experience which shapes their behavior. They are not passive in their responses in school, in fact they are most purposeful. Through Carol's participation in the class we begin to identify the students' perspective on schooling, teaching and learning.

There were frequent reminders that some students had learned that schools were a place where they failed. In the first meeting with Jeff, Rhonda and Kathy felt it was important to identify themselves as failures in maths when they introduced themselves.

Kathy: I'm Kathy and I am no good at maths.
Rhonda: My name is Rhonda and I can't do maths and I am not much better at other subjects.

This is very significant learning, one that the teacher needs to be receptive to even through informal interactions of this nature. This view of self is strong and persistent and will set limits on further progress, sadly, even when it may appear that progress is being made. This is one part of the context of schooling which is important for teachers to be aware of and to recognize. It is the context of knowing the individual student, a context which should not be too easily overlooked.

The following excerpt from Jeff's journal illustrates this point and demonstrates how powerful Julie's view of herself is and how that influences her expectations. In this case she receives a corrected mathematics test and the resultant interaction strikes a chord in Jeff's mind as he reflects on the episode later.

Journal: 16th June
Julie: What is my mark? . . . I know it will be awful.
Jeff: No Julie it was 44 out of 64. . . . that was quite good.
Julie: Oh . . . but the test was easy.
Jeff: Perhaps you are better than you think you are.
Julie: Mmm . . . I don't know . . . I don't think so.

. . . It is clear that some students accept they will not understand some areas of the work and so have no determination to fully understand everything (they give up easily). Why should they struggle and persist; not knowing some things is the normal state of affairs?

Julie, like some of her classmates in 7D, perceived school to be a place of inevitable failure. They had learned to be 'helpless'. Also, because their self-image is sensitive to the reactions of classmates it is difficult for them to change this behavior. For them, most interactions are interpreted as reinforcing this behavior. So how does one attempt to build confidence? For some, consistent good results and progress assisted. Within the variety of activities 7D experienced, some students responded to problem-solving tasks in mathematics, some to the project tasks and others to the class presentations. But it is clearly a gradual process and the gains made must be carefully built upon. Unfortunately, at least two students were limited by a low level of self-confidence throughout the year which inevitably influenced their expectations of their own ability.

The View of Self as Learner Affects Success at Learning

Rhonda's experiences have affected her view of herself as a learner. Further incidents may even reinforce the view she already has. We all know about self-esteem and its effect on learning but what surprises us is that some students intuitively recognize this lack of self-esteem for themselves. Unfortunately, recognizing it does not seem to change the situation.

> *Rhonda:* A couple of boys asked Mr Northfield a question and he said, oh something, and then went away and went up to the front and said, 'This test you went really well' or something like that and 'you're all very smart people' and just these boys said behind me, 'But not Rhonda'. So that really puts you down and makes you feel as though oh, then I mustn't be really good at it.
>
> *Carol:* But do you always believe what other people say about you?
>
> *Rhonda:* No, but it puts you down and makes you believe that you're not any good at it.

Hence, it does not take much for the small gains in self-confidence to be dashed by the responses of her peers. An opportunity for Rhonda to 'rightfully' feel successful is lost as her self-concept is so strongly influenced by others' views. In this instance, it may well be that as Rhonda's emerging view of her ability differed from that of her classmates, the resultant devaluing by her peers acted to inhibit the growth that Jeff would have hoped (and planned) for. Hence, his attempt to boost students' self-concept by praising noteworthy achievements is quietly dashed by the actions of others.

Kathy was a student who had developed a way of coping with her difficulties in understanding work. She believed that understanding was something you could or could not do. If you could not understand something then that was not likely to change.

> Like if you're [in your] last year [of Primary School], you're Grade 6, and like you're going [saying], I couldn't do this last year [then] you don't reckon you can do it this year. (Kathy)

Imagine how this must shape Kathy's view of learning. What does this suggest about how she thinks learning happens? Is education like a transmitter sending out bits of information and the student is a receiver that is supposed to just pick it up? If the receiver does not manage to pick it up the first time then that's too bad? She must certainly have been confused by Jeff's approach to teaching when his clear expectation was that he was helping students learn with understanding. It must have created some conflict in her mind when her view of learning was being continually challenged by the teaching approach in 7D. Could it be that Jeff as the transmitter kept sending out the same message, but she as a receiver was not tuned to pick it up? She had been programmed to receive the message once, she was not tuned to expect it again. If this is the case, then it is interesting to ponder how students' views of schooling develop.

Individual Context Always Affects Learning

Sometimes even single incidents can leave lasting impressions and affect the way students perceive teaching and learning. On one day Michelle described herself as 'hyper'. Students around her were intent on their problem-solving boxes in maths. Some huddled around a desk. Others worked in a relaxed manner on the floor. But not Michelle. She called out. She wandered about. She made a general nuisance of herself. Why? Her unlikely explanation to Carol was that she had been to swimming training before school that morning and that an early morning swim always made her 'hyper'. She could not sit still.

Whether this was the real reason or only one of a myriad of possibilities, something had happened to Michelle to make her 'hyper'. The teacher probably could not change that. At best, all one can do is manage the situation that is created. If twenty-five students walk into the classroom at the start of the lesson then twenty-five histories walk with them. That day. That week. That life. For the most part, teachers cannot change that. All they can do is manage it. As Section 1 of this book demonstrates, Jeff was continually attempting to manage this situation and this aspect of the context had a profound influence on the workings of the class.

During one interview, Carol had been discussing how being interested helped in learning. Linda's response demonstrated how this element of the context of learning was important. Even though being interested is helpful, it is still only one part of the puzzle. Interest may be sparked but it alone does not shape the context of learning:

Linda: It depends what kind of mood you're in. Like if we're in a sensible mood.
Carol: What affects your mood?
Linda: I don't know. If you have a bad sleep or something.

So there is always more, the context is complex and the influencing factors vary with the time of day, the mood of the students (the mood of the teacher), events from the previous lesson and so on. A myriad of possibilities, all to be managed but very difficult to control; the teacher therefore works to recognize and manage them. Donna's comments highlight the connectedness of different aspects of schooling which influence the context and reveal how her context has affected not only a particular day at school but her feelings about a whole year of school:

> *Carol:* Does it bother you that you get distracted and don't do the 'right' thing?
>
> *Donna:* Oh, sometimes, but other times . . . It depends what sort of mood I'm in. If I've had a good lunchtime I don't really care what teachers think. But if I've had a really silly lunchtime I do care. Like I think, oh no, he's going to kill me, and that sort of thing.

Then later:

> *Donna:* If you don't have friends you really feel, oh, I don't really want to go to school. Because in Grade 2 everyone turned against me and I never wanted to go to school so mum used to give me days off.
>
> *Carol:* What can give you a bad day at school?
>
> *Donna:* Friends hating you.

These observations may appear all too obvious, especially to experienced teachers. After all, a disagreement with our partner, money problems or a bad headache can affect us too and it's hard to ignore the more 'assertive' students when they are having a bad day. Yet rarely are these powerful contexts mentioned other than in passing in policy documents, curriculum materials or books that purport to advise us about how to be good teachers. Welfare coordinators deal with these issues all the time and although there is material available which could help us deal sensitively with our students' contexts, most of the time 'officially' we are dealing with Year 7s or Year 11s or Year 10s, not Kevin who has just had a fight on the oval at lunchtime, or Jackie who has been alienated by her peer group.

Students' individual contexts are inescapable and teachers learn to manage them sensitively so that their students experience success as learners. Much of the struggle new teachers face is coming to grips with the contexts that their students bring to the classroom with them. Often teachers will never even know (and how could they?) how powerfully certain experiences of learning, or even single incidents, have affected their students. Each classroom is an extremely complex, idiosyncratic setting, and creating the conditions for learning requires great skill and sensitivity (obviously a difficult task and something that is not easy to learn).

Sometimes teachers' actions inadvertently create episodes that students interpret in ways other than those intended. For example, Claire's view of an incident where she tried to show Jeff how she tackled a particular maths problem really stuck (see p. 108). It affected her to the extent that she probably would not show him how she approached a task again. His response unintentionally created an episode that would be a powerful influence on her view of what she could (and could not) divulge about her understanding of maths problems. Similarly, Rhonda's experience in Grade 5 strongly affected the way she saw herself as a learner in maths.

> It just started off that in Grade 5, my teacher used to rush ahead and never help me. He just didn't quite get the knack of it. He'd always go and give more work to people who did understand. So then you were just sort of left in the lurch and everyone else was just this much ahead of you. Bit by bit it grew and grew and grew. And that was in Grade 5 and it wasn't so bad in Grade 6 because I had a really good teacher and in Year 7 as well, but everyone is ahead. (Rhonda)

Obviously, then, there is a constant struggle for teachers as they work to improve each student's confidence so that they will become independent learners and individually have an expectation of success in their achievements. But how does one do this?

Students Take a Pragmatic Approach to School and Learning

Journal: 6th August
Thinking appears to be something I am concerned about — not part of what is and should be done at school.

That was Jeff once again reflecting on the difficulties he was experiencing. The lows commonly caused him to question his understanding of the purpose of schooling. Throughout the year he designed his lessons to promote active independent learning in the hope that it would encourage students to ask questions and actually think about thinking itself. Early journal entries continually mentioned the lack of 'excitement' and he was disappointed at how often lessons seemed 'ordinary'.

On 20th May he described how interested and involved students were in a particular lesson yet none took up his offer to take the equipment home to pursue it further. He was most disappointed. Was he expecting too much of them? Even if the subject matter is interesting, why should they do overtime? How could more schoolwork compete with a few hours playing with their friends, a date with Super Mario, Streetfighter 2 or Game Boy? What would encourage a 12 year old to actively pursue their work after hours? Is it reasonable to expect this of them?

If this is a reasonable interpretation to develop from their approach to schooling, then it appears to us that most students appear to take a pragmatic approach to their learning. They recognize it as their job at this point in their life. A few will give it all they've got, some might be workaholics, some might find it difficult to stay on the payroll. Generally, we think most do what they see as necessary to keep the bosses (parents and teachers) happy. If they enjoy the work and are interested it makes the job easier and (somedays) may lead them to feel satisfied with their own performance. But why take it home with them if they do not have to?

> Sometimes I care. Sometimes I don't. But sometimes I do all my work but then I just muck around. Like I've done all my work. The person I'm mucking around with has done all their work so he [teacher] can't say I'm disturbing other people. (Claire)

and

> *Carol:* Do you feel you don't work very hard at the moment?
> *John:* Oh. It depends what the moment is. It depends whether you're saying before the test or after the test or way before the test.
> *Nat:* Like if there's topics you already know things about.
> *John:* Like, 'time' was pretty boring. We knew that well.
> *Nat:* Yeah.
> *Carol:* Was that in maths? Oh. So do you organize the way you work and the time you spend on things according to how close the test is?
> *John:* Mainly.
> *Carol:* Do you want to explain that in a bit more detail?

John: Oh. Well, if I don't really understand it I'll work pretty hard to try and get to understand it and if I understand it really well I'll just work along at my own pace until it's about two weeks before the test and then brush up on it.

Carol: What about you Nat?

Nat: Yeah, about the same. Most of the class do.

Carol: So long as they understand it they don't work too hard unless the test's coming up.

Nat: Yeah.

John: Or they don't understand it. If they don't understand it they'll work really hard to understand it and once they do they'll just go along.

Nat and John seem to put forward a reasonable approach to work. Why would they need to apply themselves more to something they feel they have sufficiently grasped? If the system defines success as passing tests and assignments then their attitude appears to be one which will lead them to be successful. The difficulty confronting teachers (particularly for Jeff, and as is most evident in Section 1) is that if students are to adopt a different approach, the system of schooling needs to more explicitly demonstrate that other learning outcomes are important and valued. Even though many teachers and programs are indeed attempting to do this, students have already learned about the nature of school and learning, hence changing their expectations is made all the more difficult.

John: I don't really like it (school) except I go anyway.

Carol: It's a bit hard not to I guess.

John: I just go there to learn the stuff that I need to learn.

and

Gary: I don't really care.

Carol: You don't care . . .

Gary: No.

Carol: . . . about what you do in class?

Gary: Not really. 'Cos it doesn't affect you and you just do what you have to do.

Students give the impression that they wish to complete their tasks with a minimum of fuss. In some cases, to be seen as conscientious may even be undesirable. For some in 7D there was a time when this was indeed an important agenda item. They felt it necessary to correct an image of the class. They were not happy with the image being created because they were identified as being members of the 'goody goody class'.

The Goody Goody Class

In Chapter 4, Jeff's journal entry of 10th September outlined his understanding of some students' reactions to their perception of being labelled as 'good students' by their peers. At that time, they were sick of it. We now explore this episode from the students' perspective.

> *Carol:* How do you judge whether you're really smart?
> *John:* When your friends call you square.

John's comment summarizes succinctly the feelings many students had about the way their peers viewed their class, and being a 'goody goody' or 'square' was not desirable. For some this did not interfere too much with their behavior and attitude towards learning, but for others it had a powerful effect. However, one way or another, the image of being the 'goody goody' class affected everyone.

> *Fred:* We were being called in our class the square class and none of the girls liked it. So they all started to get in trouble. And that's how it happened.
> *Carol:* And what did the boys think about being called the square class. Did you mind?
> *Fred:* No. I didn't worry about it.

Fred and his friend Ken were not all that concerned about what others thought, but they did find the girls' behavior annoying. 'They can be a pain at times,' according to Ken. 'All the time,' according to Patrick. For Ken and Patrick it was the way others responded to being labelled 'square' that affected them. Kathy and Julie also found that other people 'mucking around' interfered with their work because they sometimes had to stay in.

For Georgia and Jan, being called a square hurt. They did not think of themselves as squares. Like Ken and Patrick, they also found the way it altered others' behavior to be detrimental to what happened in class.

Georgia: I liked it when we were good because you can get your work done and then you can muck around because when you're quiet — well not quiet but when you're doing questions — you get your work done and then you might get free time or something and it's just more enjoyable class time.

Carol: How do you feel about the pressure from your friends and the other kids in the class?

Jan: That's bad. Because, like say, when Fran was coming. Fran came to our class. All the kids had told her that's a goody goody class you're going into. So when Trish was coming into our class they said the same thing.

Georgia: Like I don't hang around with the same people that Jan does so we never have that and when people say you're a square because you get 100 per cent, if you want to get 100 per cent it's up to you. It's your choice.

Carol: Does it worry you that they say that to you?

Georgia: Yeah, 'cos I'm not like a square . . . I usually leave my homework really late. I mean, I get it done and if I get good marks that's up to me.

Georgia and Jan are feeling the ripple effect of the other students' behavior. Georgia is disturbed by the comments of others but she has not let it affect her attitude to her work very much (as yet). She is still concerned to get good marks. But both girls feel they have altered their behavior to a certain extent.

Jan: I want to be like them and I don't want to work because I don't want to be thought of as good and that. Like when Trish first came in I sort of felt like that.

Georgia: Yeah. 'Cos sometimes it seems really fun but then other times when you're doing it it just gets boring.

Jan: But Georgia and me sometimes muck around as well as doing our work.

We were surprised at how conscious the class members were of their so-called 'reputation' and how this affected individuals, classmates, other peers and teachers. Ken and Patrick were conscious that certain girls in the class had deliberately set out to change the class reputation from a 'goody goody' class. Other students talked openly about how the transfer of other students to their class had had an affect. Gayle and Linda explored the issue of 'reputation' in some depth and discussed how it affected them and their behavior in class.

Gayle:	We've made ourselves a reputation and teachers hold it against us.
Carol:	When you say the word reputation what exactly do you mean by that?
Gayle:	We have a bad reputation. We're naughty and stuff.
Carol:	Are you always naughty?
Gayle:	No.
Linda:	Most of the time.
Gayle:	We just started.
Linda:	We used to be really good.
Carol:	Well, why did you start to be naughty?
Gayle:	We got sick of being called the goody goody class.
Carol:	Was that the only reason?
Linda:	Well, last semester we were still settling in and stuff so we didn't want to do anything.
Carol:	What, you mean finding your way around the school and all that sort of stuff?
Linda:	And we didn't want to like get in teachers' bad books.
Carol:	But now you don't mind?
Linda:	Nup.
Gayle:	Nup.
Gayle:	Oh, 'cos I don't know. Just 'cos everyone called us the goody goody class because we didn't give the teachers crap or anything like that but now we do.
Carol:	Is it important to you how other students see you?
Linda:	More important than how the teachers see us.
Gayle:	Yeah.
Carol:	Is it? Why is that Linda?
Linda:	Because you'd rather be like friendly with the students than with the teachers.

Gayle and Linda (as well as other students) valued their peers' view of themselves more than their teachers' views. While some of these students managed to negotiate a compromise which allowed them to fit in with the expectations of both their teachers and their peers, others like Gayle and Linda did not.

Carol: Is it impossible to be friendly with your peers and also get on well with your teachers? Is that impossible?

Linda: I don't know. I haven't tried that. [She laughs]

An important contextual factor then is that quite clearly most students have a view of themselves as individuals and as a class which they wish to maintain. In this case, they did not want to be seen as 'squares' or 'goody goodies' and this led to major changes in their behavior and approach to learning. For Jeff, he had to be aware of this facet of the context and attempt to come to grips with it so that he could better manage the situation. He needed to be sensitive to both the stimulus that triggered the change in context and the response resulting from it if he was to manage and accommodate this dynamic contextual factor which had such an important influence on the students' behavior and attitude to learning. There is little doubt that the multitude of issues which comprise the context of schooling play an important role in shaping students' approach to learning.

This chapter was written to demonstrate the complex nature of the context so that students' responses to classroom situations might be better understood. They are constructing their own understanding of themselves as learners and the role of schooling and they behave according to these perceptions. In Chapter 8, 'Making Us Understand', we begin to explore the way students see learning.

Chapter 8

Making Us Understand

Overview

Students have views and perspectives which shape their responses to
events and episodes in classes. Student responses are often purposeful and can at times make more sense than the intended outcomes for
classroom activities. In this chapter we take the time to listen and learn
from the students and start to understand how purposeful their actions
can be; even though they may not always be in line with the teacher's
expectations.

Real Learning Requires the Consent of the Learner

Carol: What do you think your teachers think the most
         important thing is?
Claire: To let us understand.
Donna: To make us understand sometimes.
Claire: [laughs] Yeah.
Carol: What's the difference between to let you and to make
         you?
Donna: Sometimes you can't be bothered so they make you.
Claire: Letting you means, you know, you've got the option.
         To let you. Usually they make you.
Carol: How do they make you understand?
Claire: Keep on going through it but half the time you don't
         understand it.

As Jeff noted in his journal (20th May, p. 23), real learning requires the
consent of the learner and, as Claire and Donna so aptly point out,
even when teachers repeatedly cover work in order to *make* them
understand, it often does not work — 'half the time you don't understand'. Perhaps this is because the student 'can't be bothered', or is not
interested, or has had a bad day. Teachers may have an impressive
array of tricks in their teaching bag to promote understanding of a

given topic but they can not *make* students learn. They may be capable of making them write, or work, or be quiet, but they cannot make them understand.

> Carol: If you really have to think and think, is that bad?
> Janet: No.
> Liz: It depends what subject you're doing. In French I don't like to think.
> Carol: What about in science, does it worry you if you have to think a lot about something?
> Liz: It depends what it is.
> Janet: Yeah. If you're into it then you don't mind thinking. But if it's a really boring thing and you have to think then you don't really want to do it.

Liz and Janet appear to be talking about consent. They will consent to 'think' if they are interested. If they do not like something they prefer it to be easy, they would like to minimize the amount of thinking required. Perhaps in this case what they refer to as 'thinking' is in fact learning. They might 'do' other work but are they really learning very much from it?

One of Jeff's teaching (and assessment) strategies was to offer students the opportunity to improve their grade by re-doing a test. This was an opportunity for students to accept some responsibility for demonstrating their understanding. A student wishing to take the test again had the tasks that could be done set out on their corrected test paper. They were able to complete the nominated task and resubmit their responses in which case the second set of marks were placed in a column alongside the first result. Early in the year a few of the more confident and capable students took up this option but by the middle of the year most students were prepared to take the opportunity to demonstrate that they did really know how to complete the task. The 'make-up' test became a part of the normal class routine so that tests were not always seen as something special or different in his classes. Patsy spoke about the panic she experienced when faced with performing in a test, yet at the same time she did not mind doing a make-up test because they allowed her to have a say in it's application; she could give her consent.

> Patsy: Because you don't have to, you're not pressured into doing them so it's not like, hard to think.
> Carol: So you get to choose whether to do them or not?

> *Patsy:* Yeah. And in tests, like they're so quiet and it's not normal for our class.
>
> *Carol:* Does that make you nervous?
>
> *Patsy:* Oh, you just get used to concentrating at that noise level and it's annoying when it's so low.

and

> *Claire:* But doing the make-up test you know it's not called a test. It's called make-up. So you do it in your own time.
>
> *Donna:* And you don't think of it as a test. You think, oh yeah, it's just like a normal worksheet.

'In your own time', 'You're not pressured', 'Letting you', the very language the students use to describe what is happening is the language of choice; the language of consent.

Students Appreciate Choice and Decision-making: Developing Understanding

Many of the students interviewed raised the subject of choice at some stage during their discussions with Carol. Sometimes it was in the context of choosing a topic to investigate, sometimes choosing how they were going to investigate a topic, and for several students it was the power to decide what they needed to learn and to acknowledge what they already knew. They were telling her that they just liked to have a choice. For example, Ken and Patrick enjoyed working with their baby chicks because they designed the experiments they wanted to perform.

> *Ken:* 'Cos you get to find out things like . . . we usually [choose to] do prac. work 'cos you get to find out things for yourself.
>
> *Patrick:* And like you want to do.

Similarly, Kathy and Julie also enjoyed working with the chicks.

> *Kathy:* It was good fun. Yeah.
>
> *Julie:* You didn't have to . . . you could do what you wanted to because Mr Northfield let you do what you wanted to.

Kathy: You didn't have like a set program. Like you had to go on. You could just make up your own experiments and go ahead with them.

Gayle felt the same way about an investigative project into different brands of the same product.

Gayle: That was good.
Linda: That was OK.
Carol: Why did you like that one?
Gayle: We were like allowed to do whatever we wanted. He let us choose what we wanted to do.

The importance of students making their own decisions, being able to make a choice, is particularly highlighted when it is removed — or perhaps not offered to begin with. Jan explained her frustration when in maths Jeff (and most other maths teachers) asked students to write out the step-by-step working for their exercises. Even though she understood the reason for the directive, she found it frustrating because she knew what she was doing so would have preferred to choose not to have to show all the working out; actually quite a reasonable stance.

Jan: I know how to do it [maths working out] so what's the use if I've already done it.
Georgia: Yeah.
Jan: Yeah. See I'd like to just sort of be able to do what, not do whatever you want in maths, but like be able to like work sort of at our own, we do work at our own pace already, but sort of not having to write it down or sometimes having to write it down.
Carol: Are your talking about choosing?
Jan: Yeah, choosing what sort of things you want to do. Like he'll give you all different ones you can choose out of all different ways to learn how to do it and then you choose which you'd like to do.
Carol: And how would you? What would you base your choices on?
Jan: Sometimes just writing the answers not the question, or sometimes when you have to write the question, writing it down.
Carol: And which ones would you choose to do?

> *Jan:* Say I'm doing algebra I'd probably choose the hard-est ones. Start off with the hardest ones.
>
> *Carol:* Because the easy ones are too easy.
>
> *Jan:* No. Look at the hard ones and see if I could do them and if I couldn't do them go down to the next hard-est. Like start with the hardest to see whether I could do them.
>
> *Carol:* Oh I see. So you wouldn't have to do the easy ones if you could do the hard ones.
>
> *Jan:* Yeah, 'cos you'd already know how to do the hard ones.

The conscientious student in Jan is hesitant because she does not want her wishes to sound like laziness. But she would like to decide for herself which exercises to tackle and which to ignore. If she is confident that she can decide for herself whether she does or does not understand something, then surely she is the most qualified person to make that decision. Michelle demonstrates this point well.

> *Carol:* Do you find that you learn better if you have more choice?
>
> *Michelle:* Yeah. Because you get to think if you really need this. If you really need to know fractions then you'll do it. You'll get in front.

Unfortunately, as many teachers are aware, not all students are good at monitoring their own understanding. Perhaps they simply have not had enough practice.

> *Georgia:* Why do we have to do all the problems you set us in each topic? [in maths]
>
> *Jeff:* Mmm . . . perhaps I would be happy if you stopped when you were sure you understood the idea.
>
> *Georgia:* How would we know that?
>
> *Gillian:* What about if you never understood maths, but you get the problems right to pass the tests.

The hope that students would take responsibility for their own learning and gain a feeling of what it meant to understand an idea was always to the fore in Jeff's teaching and one of his major hopes for students' learning. One of the strategies he introduced in maths was designed to encourage students to assess their own understanding. It was organized around the notion that they could stop working on the examples in the book when they felt they were ready to do the 'key problem' on a card on the front desk (this is a major shift from the 'normal' approach to maths teaching where, for example, all of the problems on the lefthand side of the book are completed by all students, the quicker students being 'rewarded' by doing all of the problems on both sides). Jeff concluded that the individual students should be able to judge when they understood the type of problem under consideration and that they should be able to decide when they were ready to tackle the key problem. This could be regarded as a high risk teaching strategy but it certainly was one way of offering the students responsibility for, and choices in, their own learning.

Journal: 22nd October
. . . In the maths lesson I introduced the idea of doing an example at the front when they believe they understand the idea in a set of activities. It was well accepted by the kids. The hope is that it will encourage them to ask the question about understanding and make a decision about when they think they understand rather than just completing the problems that are set. An element of mastery also as they will take different amounts of time before they feel they are ready . . . an element of confidence involved . . .

Journal: 27th October
. . . The activities to be completed are a good idea but students are going to have to be encouraged to complete the requirements. Some of the better students have the confidence to tackle the task [at the front of the room]. The weaker students are still hesitant. They lack the confidence and why should they risk failure by coming out to do the task . . .

Journal: 28th October
The maths system is still working OK and some have responded well. There are some reluctant to try themselves out with the problems at the front desk. The divergence of students now creates problems at both ends of the range.

Journal: 3rd November
The maths lesson was an algebra test and some of the results were surprising. It is now clear why some students did not do the examples at the front. They were not understanding

the work and were not prepared to try themselves out at the front. This initiative will not get to these people. How do they continue to function when they do not understand? How can one find time to monitor their progress? Perhaps taking up books at random at the end of each lesson? . . . Again, the problems of varying abilities and confidence. May be able to use the problem-solving tasks to occupy other students.

From the students' perspective, the 'new' systems were not only well understood, but also appreciated. The freedom to gauge their own level of understanding offered them an opportunity to exercise their freedom of choice.

> *James:* I reckon it's good because like, say you've got an exercise the teacher sets and you know it, it gets a bit boring. You get sick of it. I reckon it's good that you just do a few of the exercise. What I mean is, just do number one or two. You just do one and then you can go on to the other things.
>
> *Robert:* Yeah, I think it's good because if you're good at one thing you can just do a couple of them, but you don't have to do the rest. Instead of spending the same time on each thing you can just do a short time but with this, the things that you don't know much about you can spend a lot more time [on].

Like James and Robert, most students responded to this system responsibly. Not all students had the confidence to make decisions for themselves, but those who did made their decisions based on their level of understanding, not on how much work they could evade. They appreciated taking some responsibility for their own learning and this was clearly borne out of the sense of trust which was an important foundation to the risks being taken by both Jeff and the students.

All of the indications from students suggested that this initiative, allowing students to make their own decisions about when (or whether) to try the task at the front desk, demonstrated that it was well understood and well accepted. However, from Jeff's perspective, perhaps the change worked too well. Ironically, this quite sensible and well-reasoned innovation led to the spread in the students' ability being further accentuated. Hence, for Jeff, students' differing levels of ability and confidence became more apparent, and this new knowledge placed an added dimension to his need for appropriate pedagogical responses.

Students Need to See the Purpose and Value of Learning Tasks

Carol: Do you need to be interested to learn?

Fran: I think it's pretty important. Like [otherwise] you think, oh yeah, I understand that and then you just forget about it.

Michelle: I mean, what's the point?

Fran and Michelle seem to be saying that for something to really make an impression on them they need to see a point to it. Fred believes 'You just go over your books and don't pay attention' if you're not interested. In other words he pretends to be learning. Claire does not even bother to pretend.

Carol: Do you learn better if you're interested.

Donna: Yeah.

Claire: If it's interesting you might pay attention. Most of the time I don't pay attention when the class starts.

Claire certainly is not sitting bright-eyed and bushy-tailed in the front row waiting to receive the signals from the learning transmitter. However, she is prepared to exert herself if she finds the lesson interesting and she can see (and accept) the underlying purpose. Unfortunately, being able to determine the interests of all of the students in a class is no simple task, especially if the students are not sure of it themselves.

Carol: So when you first came to high school you expected science to be hard, and is it?

Gayle: Well, it's not that hard.

Carol: But it's not what you expected it to be either?

Linda: It's boring.

Gayle: You know how you see in all those movies how they're always mixing chemicals and stuff and getting explosions, well I expected to do stuff like that.

Carol: You don't think electricity is science?

Gayle: Yeah, it is except . . .

Linda: It just hasn't got much to do with it.

Carol: Much to do with what?

Linda: Science. I don't know why but . . .

Carol: Well, what would you have in science? Chemicals, but what else?

Linda: I don't know. Just. I don't know. Chemicals and stuff. Mixing stuff.

Carol: Mixing things.

Gayle: Stuff like wounds [referring to a lesson where they made fake wounds with a play dough type mixture which they prepared].

Carol: So is that science?

Linda: Not really.

Gayle: Not really.

Linda: I don't know.

Carol: What about the way it turns from a claggy thing to a lump of dough. A ball. Is that science — when you put the heat on it?

Gayle: Sort of.

Carol: Sort of. What about when you did the tests with the material?

Gayle: That was science.

Linda: That was boring.

Carol: So is science only things that are not boring?

Linda: Everything that we do seems to be boring. My parents always said, 'You'll enjoy science, that'll be fun,' and stuff, but it's boring.

Carol: It's boring. Well, what would you like to do in science. What wouldn't be boring?

Gayle: Mixing chemicals.

Linda: Making slime.

Gayle: Dissecting stuff.

Linda: I don't want to do that.

It would be difficult for a teacher to determine Gayle's and Linda's interests in science and, during her interviews, Carol found that several other students also had ideas similar to those expressed by these two. Therefore, in some cases, students' ideas about a subject may make it even more difficult for the teacher to make the purpose and value of learning tasks clear and acceptable to students. A similar situation may arise when the students' and teachers' understanding of particular learning tasks or activities differ. In some cases, it may be that the difference in opinion is as a result of a lack of communication, in others it may be that the two positions are simply different. This was most likely the case with The Story of Velcro. Jeff saw it as a worthwhile activity. However, the students had a different point of view and their response to the lesson demonstrated this to him. They did not see the purpose or value in the task. Perhaps to them it was because 'it was not science'.

One clue many students offered about what they found purposeful in learning was hands-on tasks. John and Nat felt that because they were interested in practical work that they would put more effort into their work; they would try harder.

Carol: Why do you like hands-on things better?

John: 'Cos there's no written work. That's one point. And mostly the hands-on stuff is fun and interesting.

Carol: Do you think you learn more that way or with the written work?

John: Oh, you learn more that way because lots of people are interested in the hands-on.

Nat: I think when you're having fun you learn more because if you're real bored you might be a bit slack. And you won't try hard.

John: Fall asleep.

Building on this view of interest and involvement, James and Robert believed that hands-on tasks helped them to learn better because they were able to see what happened and were able to make their own conclusions and judgments; seeing is believing.

James: . . . Because when you actually do it you actually know. Like with the notes you read off the page and you can read how they say it happens and that but if you actually do the experiment you can actually see how it happens and make your own judgments rather than setting up [to find out] another person's.

Carol: So when you make your own judgments do you worry about whether they're going to be right or not?

James: Mr. Northfield says in science if you do an experiment you can't really be wrong because each experiment is different. Like if you're using chemicals you could put a bit more or that. So when you do it you've got your own answers.

Carol: Do you like having your own answers, Robert?

Robert: Oh yeah. You just know they're correct. You know you can't get them wrong.

James: You know that you've done it. Even though it might

not turn out the same as everyone else, the fact that
yours turned out. You know it happened.

An important aspect to James' and Robert's dialogue is the way they
seem to have been influenced by Jeff's view of practical/laboratory
work. They do not appear to be aimlessly completing exercises to redis-
cover a scientific concept but, more so, to better understand the concept through their own experience. There is a clear purpose to these
learning tasks and they recognize the value in them. In a similar vein,
perhaps that is what Ken is reinforcing when he discusses the value of
learning for himself.

Ken:	Things that aren't fun are just things that get dictated to you and you have to cross them off sheets and stuff.
Patrick:	Work stuff.
Ken:	You get all cooped up.
Carol:	So you like to do things?
Ken:	Yeah. Like to find out things for ourselves.
Carol:	Do you think you learn it better that way?
Ken:	Yeah, 'cos then it sinks into your head. 'Cos otherwise you're just sort of writing it down and then at the end of the year the paper will just get chucked out. If you go outside or inside and then find out things for yourself it'll actually stick in your brain.

If the students are then able to see the purpose and value of a learning
task, then they might more whole-heartedly apply themselves to the
activity. However, as already noted, the context of a situation and the
ability to spark students' interest are also important. It is not possible
to outline a protocol for learning which can account for all of these all
of the time. Sometimes unexpected opportunities play an important
part in learning. Hence for the teacher, being continually receptive
and responsive to students' interests, needs, concerns and reactions is
vital.

Journal: 29th October
. . . Certainly this was not a lesson [science] where much progress
was made. A lot of preparation/thought which resulted in a
disappointing response . . . limited outcomes. [Students were
working with electric circuit boards and asked to connect circuits which solved certain problems.] Again my disappointment

was expressed and there seemed to be some support. The 'critical mass' to take the edge off a lesson or activity is quite small. Three or four opting out can reduce effectiveness especially when they distract others. So we again faced the complexity of context and daily variations in students and the opportunities were not successfully used . . . Consider Fran. Midway through the lesson she expresses no interest in electricity, 'It is boring, I don't understand anything.' She goes to the circuit boards and successfully sets up the circuit which addresses the problem. She is excited. She admits she doesn't know why she did not try. It is interesting and she has a good sense of achievement. Perhaps there is [only] so much energy that can be invested in the school day and we expect efforts throughout the day.

For Fran, a breakthrough, for most of the others, an activity which did not appear to fulfil its potential. For Jeff, some disappointment that his carefully planned lessons and activities had not coincided with students' readiness to learn. Yet, despite this, an unmistakably fine outcome arose from an unexpected opportunity. But, on this occasion, Jeff was listening and responding to the opportunity in this classroom context, and as a result Fran gains a sense of achievement.

From a teacher's perspective, there may be some frustration at the fine line between a successful activity and a disappointment. Students may simply not be ready, or an activity may not be introduced carefully enough. Combined with this is a recognition that there is a critical mass of students that appear to be able to shape the acceptability of an activity; an important realization. The teacher needs to persevere as it takes an effort to get students past a threshold just to try an activity and experience some success. Do they fear failure and find it difficult to take risks? Fran's experience was not rare. Different students gained satisfaction when they made an attempt at different times throughout the year.

Interest appears to be associated with so many things: a narrow stereotyped view of science and anticipation of how it 'should be' in the school setting; an expectation of possible failure when an activity does not work for them, or a fear that doing something might lead to further learning demands. Hence, many students appear to have learnt that they are unlikely to understand, so they make little effort. This may be compounded by a small group of students exerting a peer group influence; or a mood in the class brought about by a demanding or difficult previous lesson; or perhaps a teacher who was not sufficiently sensitive to the class and missed signs and opportunities as he moved through his agenda. If so, then it is little wonder that an initial response is often, 'Boring; what use is this?' It is a response borne of many interrelated and connected events, episodes and experiences. Yet, as Fran's transcript demonstrates, under the right conditions this response may be challenged and the purpose and value of a learning task might be recognized, and result in successful learning outcomes.

Chapter 9

Learning is Difficult

Overview

From the students' perspective it is not easy to come to terms with demands for thinking and understanding. Students see both of these aspects of learning as a 'teacher expectation', neither of these expectations fit easily with their already well-formed perceptions of the personal and institutional demands of school.

Monitoring Understanding

Students have well-developed ideas about success and learning. They have been shaped throughout their years of schooling and they inevitably influence their expectations of teaching and their approach to learning. This chapter attempts to explore how students define understanding and how this might be linked to their view of success at school.

In the cartoons a light bulb appears over the character's head when struck by a brilliant idea. For many reasons this image is familiar to us, not the least being because it does sometimes appear that something that was difficult to make sense of suddenly becomes clear, almost as if a light was turned on. Rhonda also identifies with this image.

Carol: Do you always know when you understand something?

Rhonda: Yeah, because you've got this thing in your head that goes, 'Oh, I understand that.' It's like a little man turning a light on in your head.

Like many other students, this description of understanding as the way something just 'clicks' is quite common. However, some students also experience times when the bulb is lit, but the light dims as the understanding is not fully realized. Patsy described this as:

> 'Cos like if you think you understand something, but when you go up to the teacher you go [and say] what you thought. It's sometimes wrong. It's really annoying when you think you understood it and it's not right. (Patsy)

Therefore, the ability to monitor one's understanding is important, especially for students whose self-confidence does not need the ordeal of being tested in the type of situation outlined by Patsy. Hence, students need to develop ways of monitoring their understanding if they are to 'manage' the learning demands in school. There is no one monitoring mechanism, but the range of mechanisms students develop, and the degree of sophistication associated with them, varies from student to student. If teaching is to foster understanding, then recognizing how students monitor their understanding is important.

> *Carol:* How do you know if you don't understand something?
> *Fred:* You can't do the work.
> *Gary:* If you can't do it then you don't know what you have to be doing.
> *Carol:* And if you are doing it does that mean you understand it?
> *Gary:* Oh, it depends.
> *Fred:* It would.
> *Gary:* You might be checking in the back of the book or something.

For Fred, and many other students, there may be little distinction between doing and understanding. Therefore, developing a 'way of knowing' can be a crucial element in learning for understanding. Some students solved this problem by relying on others.

> *Carol:* Do you know when you understand something?
> *Gayle:* Well, if we go back and try it out or something and go and show Mr Northfield to see if it's right or whoever the teacher is and she says no, then you don't understand.
> *Carol:* You don't know yourself, you have to ask somebody else.
> *Gayle:* If he says it's right then you show him how you did it.
> *Carol:* And when he says it's not, does that help?
> *Gayle:* Yeah, he would say it's not and then he'd show us how to do it.

Gayle does not seem to have processes for monitoring her own understanding. She appears to rely on the teacher to confirm or deny her ability to do the work and, in this case, she seems to be suggesting that 'doing' and 'understanding' are the same. Like Gayle, Fran relies on others and demonstrates how, for her, doing and understanding are interchangeable. Michelle however has clearly developed a distinction between the two and can test her understanding when she applies her 'Can I follow it?' approach:

> *Fran:* Because you do one of the questions and you ask them is that the right answer and if they say yes then you think, yes I understand it. I got it right.
>
> *Carol:* So are you saying to me that you're relying on someone else to help you know whether you understand it? Can you do it all by yourself without asking someone if it is right?
>
> *Michelle:* If they say you do this, then you do that and you can follow it, well then you understand it. But if they say something and you just think, huh, what did they just say then [you don't understand it].

Michelle's response suggests that she actively processes information as she receives it to check her understanding as she works through a task. But Fran appears to complete tasks and then determine whether or not she understands the process by ascertaining whether or not she arrived at the right answer; the steps in between do not lead to understanding, getting the correct answer is understanding. This is an interesting difference in approach between these two students and perhaps a demonstration of an increased level of sophistication of monitoring one's own learning.

Other ways of monitoring understanding were suggested by Claire and Donna. In both cases, they used other resources to check on their level of understanding and they did so in quite active ways. This is quite a move forward from relying on being told where a mistake may have been made, they show how they work things out for themselves. Donna even had a name for this process.

> *Claire:* ... [or] Else I just get the answer out of the back of the book and see how they got it.
>
> *Donna:* Yeah, backtrack it.
>
> *Claire:* And then do another one.

Carol:	Is that what you call it — backtracking? How do you do backtracking?
Donna:	Well you just, like if you don't get the question, you go to the back of the book and try to work out how you got that question. Times it, divide and everything. But if you can't get that answer then you go ask someone.
Carol:	Do you do that a lot? Backtrack. Is it helpful?
Donna:	Mmmm. It is. Because with Time [a topic they had done in maths] I didn't really get half of that so I had to keep looking at the back of the book and backtracking.

Donna is describing a process for checking more than the 'just arriving at the right or wrong answer'. She is demonstrating how she works her way through a problem so that she can be sure that she knows what she is doing and can self-correct or self-learn. Notice she does not mention asking for help, especially from the teacher, she is confident and content to monitor her understanding of the process by working back through it. Another example of this approach was offered by Julie.

Julie:	Well, Kathy gave me the answer to one of them and . . . then I tried to work it out again and I got that answer. Like when he sets, when he puts say three-quarters of this that's easy, but when he puts it in a sentence I just can't figure it out, it's harder.
Carol:	Mmm. Do you look up the answer in the back of the text book?
Kathy:	Yep. Sometimes.
Carol:	And how does that help?
Kathy:	Well, if Mr Northfield says you can do it you check your book.
Carol:	But I mean, how does it help your understanding?
Julie:	Well. One day I looked in the book and I saw what the answer was. It gave me the question. Like do expansion on this question, on these five questions. But you don't know what 'expansion' means. And so I looked in the back for the first one and then I understood what it meant when it showed me the answer.

This approach can obviously be quite sophisticated, perhaps especially so in Julie's case for, as she initially described it, her use of an answer from Kathy was actually during a test. She was using the answer to backtrack. Kathy's answer helped her work out how to do the questions for herself. She knew how to develop her understanding of the process in quite a confident and sophisticated way. This suggests that she must have been asking herself questions about the work so that she could find the missing link(s) in her puzzle of understanding. John was quite conscious of this questioning process and volunteered some of the questions he asked himself in order to monitor his understanding.

John: . . . If you're doing experiments and you do it a couple of times and it all turns out fine you can say, 'Oh, yeah, I know how to do that.' And if it doesn't turn out fine you say, 'Where did I go wrong?' then go back and try and do it again.

Carol: What other sorts of questions do you have in your head?

John: 'Why isn't this working?' mainly, or sometimes when I fluke it, 'Why is this working?'

John is quite consciously monitoring his own understanding. Even when he 'flukes' an answer he wants to know how and why it has happened: a very useful strategy to monitor 'how well he knows'. So what happens if the problem cannot be solved alone? How do students obtain help and how do they view this step in developing understanding?

Asking for Help

John: He [Mr Northfield] understands most of our questions when we ask him.

Nat: Sometimes you've got your hand up and he doesn't really come.

John: It takes him about ten minutes to get from one side of the room to the other.

Carol: Why is that?

John: Because all of the other people come up and ask him questions.

These students obviously recognize the difficulties created when the teacher is trying to help each student individually. There may be a problem that is immediate for the student, but there is a wait-time that influences the teacher's response, a wait-time during which the teacher categorizes, prioritizes, and individualizes the learning demands of the students. This constant juggling must make it difficult to respond appropriately to all students all of the time. For example, Rhonda described her view of how teachers sometimes respond when she asks for help, 'They just sort of look at you as though you don't know what you're talking about'. One wonders what the look means from the teacher's perspective and whether Rhonda's perception matches the teacher's intent. In some cases perhaps it does, but we would suggest that on many occasions it is more likely that the teacher is attempting to juggle the demands of the particular query along with all of the others being posed at the time. Considering all of this, it is then not unreasonable to see that even if students feel that the teacher does understand where they need help, they might find the whole undertaking arduous and not always worth the effort.

All of this is exacerbated if the student is struggling and is concerned about voicing their difficulties in front of the class, especially if everyone else seems to have the task in hand.

Julie: Sometimes it's a bit embarrassing though 'cos with the teachers . . .

Kathy: Everyone . . .

Julie: If someone doesn't understand something while Mr Northfield's telling them he goes, 'Does anybody else think . . .'

Kathy: Not understand . . .

Julie: Yeah. And then no one puts their hand up.

Kathy: And you think, oh no, what if I put my hand up and everyone laughs at me?

Carol: But do you think sometimes a lot of people don't understand?

Julie: Yeah, because . . .

Kathy: Yeah.

Julie: . . . in English Miss is, um, very . . . she goes, 'Does anyone not understand?' and no one put their hand up and then she goes, 'Well, then it's all right . . .'

Kathy: 'Start working,' and all these people put their hands up saying . . .

Julie: 'I don't understand.'

Carol: Why do you think you get embarrassed about saying you need help?

Kathy: Because, like, people think, oh God she's so dumb. She doesn't even understand.

Julie: And if you're not like with the people like Linda and

all them — don't tell them I said this — but when
you're with them well . . .

Kathy: Will the class get to listen to this?

Carol: No. It's private.

Julie: Well, if you're in Linda's group then it's all right because they don't tease you.

Kathy: Yeah.

Julie: But if you're not with them then they tease you.

Carol: Even if they don't understand themselves?

Kathy: I don't know. Sometimes they just tease you.

Julie: Well, Linda and Fran and all that they always seem to
like understand it and like the teacher goes, 'Who
doesn't understand' and like everyone looks around.
You put up your hand and Linda goes, 'God!' and then
they whisper to each other.

It would seem reasonable to assume that if students are having trouble
with their work that they will ask the teacher for help, then the teacher
will do his best to clarify the task/content at hand. But this is not always
the way it happens. There may be many factors which hinder this, not
least of which is the dynamics of the relationships within the classroom.
Peer ridicule can be a very powerful disincentive. The views expressed by the students above demonstrate how so many other factors
influence learning. What must it be like then for a teacher who is
intent on helping students learn with understanding? So many things
make it difficult for students to take the risks necessary to express
their view and to explore their lack of understanding in a meaningful
way.

It is Difficult to be a Good Learner

Throughout the year there was ample evidence that students were aware
of what could be regarded as good learning behaviors. On several
occasions a loaded camera was introduced for students to take photographs of activities which could be used to show people good learning
in their classroom. The photographs were used for later discussion
using prompts such as, 'What is going on here?' and 'Why did you take
this photograph?'

All of the students in 7D participated, taking four or five photographs and passing the camera on until the film was complete in
each lesson. This task was almost always taken seriously and the

Figure 1: Good learning behaviors

---

1   Ask the teacher when they do not understand.
2   Does extra work to make sure they can understand and do the task.
3   Suggests new ideas and thinks of other explanations.
4   Asks questions about new work.
5   Tries to link new ideas to other work in school and experiences at home.
6   Checks all work to see that everything has been done.
7   Makes sure they are clear about what they have to do and why they have to do it.
8   Thinks about an idea and plans to answer before giving an answer.
9   Takes care in presenting their work and making their notes.

---

follow-up discussion revealed interesting and often surprising perspectives on learning.

On several occasions students were asked to write responses to questions such as: What do you need to do to improve your results in the future? and, If you get a bad result on a maths test, what are the most likely reasons? and, What are some things people can do to help them learn better?

The responses and follow up to the last question reveal a great deal about students' perceptions of learning in schools. As Jeff noted in his journal (Chapter 3, 2nd July p. 30), having the students respond to a list of good learning behaviors was one way of determining their perspective on their approach to learning. The nine good learning behaviors (Figure 1), derived from the work of teachers (Baird and Northfield, 1992), were given to the students. They then chose two they felt they would like to respond to from the list. The first four good learning behaviors attracted most responses from the students. Ten students chose to discuss the first good learning behavior and provided the following difficulties in adopting what they had offered as a good way to learn better:

I am scared to tell the teacher . . . you might be the only one.

I feel I am wasting other people's time.

Everyone else understands . . . they laugh at me.

I will get embarrassed. (Repeated in a similar way by 4 students)

It makes you feel (nervous) to ask questions.

I have my hand up for too long.

I can never be bothered.

Nine students responded to the difficulties of carrying out the second good learning behavior:

> . . . you get sick of doing the task.

> don't want to understand.

> Will never understand anyway.

> I spend extra time but then we have moved onto other things.

> I have no time . . . too many things to do. (3 students)

> When I'm finished the set work in class I'm [relieved] and don't feel like or want to do any extra work.

The third good learning behavior was discussed by three students:

> It is difficult because I'm not sure if the ideas are good or make any sense.

> Someone else will always suggest a better idea than me . . . they will think I am silly.

> Someone else has suggested it before me.

The possibility that students should ask questions about new work (the fourth good learning behavior) was selected for comment by five students:

> I will feel stupid in front of my friends.

> I try to wait until someone else asks.

> I feel stupid.

> People will think I am dumb.

> It's hard to do this because if no one else wants to ask, then you feel like maybe you shouldn't and you feel sometimes it's a dumb question.

In general the students' responses reveal two underlying reasons for their difficulty in following recognized good learning behaviors. Firstly, there is the concern about peer (and teacher) reactions when/if learning initiatives are taken. Few wish to provide opportunities for others to think of them as 'silly' or 'dumb' and therefore prefer not to take the risk of exposing their understanding (or lack of understanding) publicly. Secondly, confidence, or more so lack of confidence, is an overriding concern as the following illustrate:

I put myself down.

I am worried that I will not know enough and they will find out.

I lack self-confidence.

With these responses in mind it is easy to see why the classroom may not be an environment to support the forms of more independent and active learning that Jeff had been working towards. Despite even his best efforts much more would have to be done to build sufficient confidence and trust in those students who expressed their concerns in this area.

The students knew the purpose that underpinned Jeff's teaching and there were times when they acknowledged this in response to an activity:

We know . . . you are trying to make us think.

But it was less frequent that students would engage wholeheartedly in the activity and Jeff was often reminded of their expectations of him as their teacher:

You are supposed to know and tell us the answers.

Thinking may have been on his agenda, but students generally remained wary and did not have the confidence to become too involved at this stage of their schooling. When asked to state the one thing they could do to improve their performance, the majority of students identified 'listening more carefully to instructions and the teacher' as their first priority.

It seems then that the students are carrying with them two views which continually impact on their learning behavior in the classroom. One in which understanding may be a useful and valuable way of 'knowing' schoolwork better (hence the development of monitoring mechanisms) and one in which trying to understand is associated with risks that are too great to contemplate or suffer. With this in mind it is interesting to consider how students viewed success at school and how these issues influenced these views.

What Does it Mean to be Successful?

The students offered a range of responses to questions about their own, and their teachers', perceptions of success. However, Fred's account went straight to the heart of the matter when he offered his unequivocal definition.

Fred: I think James is defining successful.
Carol: What is James?
Fred: A straight A student.
Carol: What do you think your teachers think successful is?
Fred: James.

Even though Fred's definition is ascribed to the personal success of James, the intent is still clear, it is akin to 'getting good grades', and that is also how most other students defined success. John's response 'getting high grades really', is indicative of this view. However, Liz offered a more personal understanding when she said, 'getting the best set of marks *you* can get', she then went on to explain:

Liz: Well, not just marks. Just say there's one really smart
           person in the class and there's one that isn't so smart,
           the smart person achieves as much as he could which
           is different to what the other person could achieve.
Carol: Uh huh. So it's a very personal thing. What about for
           you, Janet, what do you think success at school is?
Janet: Trying to do things the best you can get.

Liz and Janet hint at an understanding of success that is measured against their own ability rather than that of others. Therefore it was interesting to hear Fred's epitome of success, James, describe his view of success.

Like you might get an A in a subject that you're not really good at. If you achieve it then that's what I reckon success is. If you try really hard and you really want to get there and when you get your report you get a B or something and the last time you got a C or something, then that would be success. (James)

Perhaps James's comments reflect more truly the sentiments of his peers. Success is about personal achievement. But this achievement is still measured by others (teachers usually) with grades. The students are caught between two conflicting positions. That of personal achievement measured against oneself, and that of achievement in comparison to others. Measuring these achievements though is largely being drawn from that which is done *to* the students *through* assessment. Therefore, two conflicting messages may be being received by students. On the one hand a teacher may talk about understanding as being an important part of teaching and learning, but on the other the judgments about success are being made in terms of grades. In many ways, the grades then denote success or failure and eschew comparisons between students which are counterproductive in terms of an individual determining success as a gain in understanding measured against oneself. This interpretation of success in schooling is not necessarily new for many teachers. However, we were quite surprised with the response Carol gained when she asked Gayle and Linda what they thought a teacher's view of success might be.

> *Linda:* What we think, they probably think successful is stuff like understanding.
> *Gayle:* Yeah. Being able to understand.
> *Carol:* Ah . . . right [just to be sure she was hearing them correctly she continues] What about teachers, what would they think it is?
> *Gayle:* That's what they think.
> *Linda:* Yeah.
> *Carol:* Being able to understand. And to you it's getting good grades?
> *Linda:* Yeah.
> *Gayle:* Yeah.

We would argue then that Jeff's approach to teaching these students had conveyed to them that learning with understanding was important and that it was something which he valued. The influence of this view on his students seems clear:

> *Nat:* Mr Northfield says that . . .
> *John:* If you can understand something . . .
> *Nat:* And do it, then whether you get all As or Bs and Cs it doesn't matter.

and

> I reckon success to him [Mr Northfield] would be if he got you to understand it even if you didn't get the test all right. I think

if at the end, even if you didn't get the answers, if you'd really tried then he would think that was success. (James)

and

You don't *have* to understand it but I reckon you have to tell him if you don't understand it. (Michelle)

This is indeed interesting, but it is also tempered by the mixed messages the students are receiving at the same time. A teacher may be telling his students that he values understanding and effort but to the students he is ostensibly valuing their efforts with tests and grades. Hence Ken and Patrick's comments:

Ken: If you're satisfied with what you've done and . . .

Patrick: If you think that you've done the best that you can do and you've got what you think you deserve for it and you feel proud of yourself.

Ken: Yeah. And feel proud of yourself.

Patrick: When you get a mark and the teacher's given you a bad mark . . .

Ken: And you don't feel happy with yourself even though you've put in your best thing.

So despite the student's internal sense of satisfaction and success, the external measure (teacher's assigned grade for the work) operates in a manner which may be counter to the learning which the student may have valued and defined as successful. Therefore, writing and tests become valued by the students even if much of the real learning takes place in other ways; such as the hands-on, doing situations described earlier. This dilemma is most apparent with Fred who seems confused about what is (or should) actually be valued. He does not consider science practicals/laboratory experiments as work, even though this is what he enjoys the most, and says he learns most from, 'No it's not school work. It's prac.' It must be difficult for him to pay attention and concentrate on learning when what he enjoys is not schoolwork. One wonders what he has to do to learn schoolwork.

If these students' views of success are a guide, learning schoolwork must surely be made all the more difficult if they are expected to learn for understanding. They certainly exist in a world which is difficult to safely or easily traverse. Little wonder they develop coping mechanisms which conflict with their views of good learning behaviors.

Chapter 10

A Focus on the Teacher

Overview

The interactions and learning demands which students experience are inevitably interpreted and reshaped in response to their understanding of schooling. Their responses can be understood when their perspectives are revealed. In this chapter we begin to explore the students' understanding of their teacher.

Mr Northfield Again

In accepting the teaching allotment of science, maths and home group, Jeff considered it would offer certain advantages. For him, one teacher taking the students for a significant amount of time could mean opportunities to link mathematics ideas with science ideas and even home group topics. There was also the possibility of working for more extended periods of time with particular tasks. Science lessons could be replaced by time for mathematics if interest in an activity warranted this. In addition to this flexibility it seemed that a longer period of time with students would lead to better understanding of their development and allow more support to be provided across the wide area of their schooling. Although these potential advantages were clear to Jeff, they were not always appreciated, or shared, by his students.

Fran:	We have maths and science and homegroup with the same teacher so it's like we've got Mr Northfield again. We've got Mr Northfield again.
Michelle:	And we've got Mr Northfield again. And we've got Mr Northfield again.
Carol:	I suppose at least you get to know each other.
Michelle:	Yeah, I suppose.
Fran:	Also that if you misbehave in one class he takes it out on you in the next as well.
Fran:	Yeah. He makes you . . .

Michelle: It doesn't make him know that you've been naughty but . . .

Carol: But you're still there basically aren't you?

Fran: And your punishment is still there. And your naughtiness is still in his mind.

Carol: Do you find that when you go from one class to another that you can start again?

Michelle: Yeah.

Fran: Yeah. Besides, you get a little bit of a break in between.

Fran and Michelle seem to be implying that Jeff is only human (*albeit* of the teacher variety) and being human he cannot forget the 'naughtiness' of his students when classes are held one after another. Having the same teacher for two subjects and home group means that it is not so easy to make a fresh start with the change of lessons, as is the case when each subject is taught by a different teacher.

Fran and Michelle's view about 'naughtiness' was also raised by Jan. She recognized that not only was it likely the behavior of the students carried over from one lesson to the next, the behavior of the teacher could also influence his approach, simply having the bell sound the end of the lesson did not mean that his mood would change.

Because if you do something wrong in one class then he'll get cranky with you in the second one . . . (Jan)

When asked whether they found Mr Northfield different in any way in maths and science many students raised what to them was a concern; having the same teacher for more than one subject. While a couple of students found it useful having the same teacher for more than one subject, they could often continue working on a task rather than switching off as soon as the bell went, most students found that having the same teacher for two subjects had definite disadvantages. They had no difficulty voicing their opinions.

Fred: Sometimes we've got maths and science like a double period and he lets us do double maths or double science.

Gary: Yeah, it's good with that but sometimes you have to hand it in. You might have period one and then period six and you can work on it at lunchtime but you can't do that if you've got him again straight after period one.

Fred: Bull!

Gary: You can't!

Robert: In a way it's good because like you can do more stuff on the same thing. Like if you run out of time on maths and you've got science next then you can do a bit of maths in science.

Robert recognizes an advantage in being able to continue with a task once he has started it rather than being disturbed by the change of subjects. However, not all students appreciated it when Jeff allowed them to continue with a science task in maths or vice versa. Fran and Michelle wanted a definite break between subjects.

Michelle: If we haven't finished it we do the work from the class before. And then he'll go 'Right, you can finish off what you were doing in the other class.'

Carol: Don't you like doing that?

Michelle: You need to have a rest from science or maths or something like that.

Fran: Like we get sick of doing maths and then science because we know what we're going to do.

Liz also dislikes doing maths in science or science in maths. She likes the structure and order that the timetable offers. She finds comfort in knowing exactly what she is going to be doing next and sticking to it.

Liz: I prefer to have a different teacher for every subject because sometimes Mr Northfield he mixes science with maths and like he goes, 'We'll just finish this science thing in maths' and it's really confusing. 'Cos you get all muddled up.

Carol: But at primary school you used to have the same teacher for every subject. Why is it different now?

Liz: Because we didn't have certain times that you'd have certain things. They'd just go, 'We're doing maths now, get your maths books out.'

Other students found that having the same teacher for different subjects meant that either they got sick of him or he got sick of them.

Considering they had only recently left primary school where they had the same teacher nearly all day, the secondary school approach of different teachers for different subjects seems to have quickly influenced their thinking.

> You get sick of him after a while. Like you've had him for a 45 minute unit and you've just gone back for another 45 minute unit. And it sort of gets a bit boring having the same teacher. (Ken)

It may well be that by this stage in their schooling, students are becoming more adept at coping in their environment, perhaps they do not like it when their approach to the routine within their workplace is altered. By Year 7 they are old hands at the business of schooling, they are mid-career workers. For seven years they have been operating in a school environment and, like any worker, throughout that time they have developed views about their workplace: the role of the teacher, their own roles as students and the nature of school. They know their workplace and its expectations and changes can be unsettling.

The role of the teacher maybe quite clear to them as they have had ample time and experience responding to their teacher's directions.

> *Carol:* [Chatting about some of the work the students were doing.] Why do you think you were doing that?
> *Gary:* I don't know. Because Mr Northfield told us to.
> *Carol:* Did you wonder at the time why he'd asked you to do that?
> *Fred:* 'Cos he's the teacher.

Although most students' perceptions of teachers are not as extreme as Patrick's view, 'They're cruel . . . Mr Northfield's the exception', they have developed beliefs about how teachers function in the classroom and how they as students understand and perceive this role. Inevitably, not all of these views will be positive, but they have developed through an ongoing series of interactions in the past. So when Jeff lightheartedly told his students that their brains were younger than his, his hope that this would encourage them to see that they could work things out for themselves, and that he expected them to try to do so, was not viewed that way by some of his students.

> I don't like the way he keeps on saying, 'Oh, you're smarter than me. . . . your brains are younger' and all this. (Georgia)

They interpreted this differently. A difference shaped by years of experiences that gave them a different slant on the meaning. In some cases they have learnt to apply their own interpretation to events, such that they make assumptions, assumptions that in many cases may well be correct, but in others can be misleading.

Carol: Do you find Mr Northfield different?
Fred: He's sarcastic. He walks around saying, 'All you kids are smarter than me.'
Carol: I think he's just making a joke with you.
Gary: No. He thinks it 'cos he always says it.

Some students have learnt to cope in their workplace by accepting that some aspects are simply to be endured. So even when teachers are doing their best to create an environment which is challenging, interesting and fun, the students' learned response is to adopt a coping strategy for something which they assume needs to be endured.

Julie: . . . But I reckon it's better for us to find out for ourselves than him tell you 'cos everyone goes, 'Oh, Mr Northfield's talking. This is really boring,' and then they don't listen.
Carol: But someone needs to tell you what these words mean, don't they?
Julie: Yeah. [But] No one wants to listen to the teachers.
Kathy: So if you find out for yourself it's better.

Julie and Kathy demonstrate that their response to the teacher talking is to apply one of their coping strategies. Their experience suggests that when teachers talk it gets in the way of them finding things out for themselves, therefore they do not need it, so they assume it will be boring and they tune out. All of this is triggered by the teacher calling attention to something he considers they need to know. Fred certainly encapsulates this view in his rapid-fire response to Carol attempting to understand why he thinks some things are boring.

Fred: He gives us boring stuff to do.
Carol: Why do you think it's boring?
Fred: 'Cos he gives it out.

John is quite articulate, even cynical in his view of teachers and how they organize the activities of the classroom. Although Jeff hoped to foster initiative, participation and decision-making with his students, he is fighting an uphill battle with someone who has the attitude that John demonstrates here. One might also wonder how John developed this attitude.

John: . . . so we think, oh, we've got an idea to do this [work- ing on a problem] except we have to do this [work through it using the teacher's suggested approach] so we'll do this [the teacher's way] and then do the other one [our way] just for the hell of it — even though we're not supposed to.

Carol: Have you ever suggested to him [Mr Northfield] that you'd like to do something a different way?

John: No. Not really.

Carol: Why, what do you think he'd do?

John: Don't know. Probably just say we might try that next time.

Carol: Is that what teachers usually do?

Nat: Yeah. They say we might try that next time.

Carol: And do they?

Nat: No.

Carol: Why do you think that happens? Why is it that it is mostly the teachers who think up what to do and when the students have ideas they don't normally get to do them?

John: Mainly because the teachers think, they've also got ideas of their own, they think, 'I've got a good idea so we'll make them do this.' And on the hard ones they think, 'Oh, I can't think of anything [for the students to do, so then they say to the students] Here, think up something you can all do with this?'

John has not bothered to make any suggestions to Jeff because he believes Jeff's answer to any such request would be a foregone conclu- sion. Regardless of Jeff's intentions, many students' existing prejudices about teachers' motives are quickly triggered by classroom events; events which have shaped their thinking over many years. It is little wonder, then, that they respond and act according to these preconceived ideas.

Differing Perceptions of Classroom Events

As section 1 (Chapters 1–5) demonstrates, Jeff was continually con- cerned about encouraging students to think and to see that there was not always one right answer or only one way of doing things. However, Jan and Georgia were not quite sure what to make of this.

Georgia:	. . . with English what you think is more . . . what you actually think is usually right because people have different opinions but with maths and science there's only one way.
Jan:	You've got to have it right.
Carol:	Do you have to have it right in science?
Jan:	I mean, like there's one answer for most things.
Georgia:	Yeah.
Jan:	But Mr Northfield doesn't think that sort of. He says everybody has their own answer but there is really in maths only one answer.
Carol:	What do you feel about that — Mr Northfield saying that everybody has different answers in science.
Jan:	I like it.

Jan and Georgia appear to have some grasp of the notion that Jeff has been trying to portray, but their existing views of science and maths get in the way of them fully accepting Jeff's approach. Claire however is very different. Her view of how she needs to operate in the classroom is clear and definite. Her perception of Jeff's response to certain events has taught her not to openly demonstrate that she does do things differently; she thinks that is not what Jeff wants to see.

Claire:	But with Mr Northfield you've got to do it his way. His way is the right way. There's no other way but his way. Like when I was trying to explain the way I did a maths problem I got in trouble. He said, 'How did you do it?' and so I showed him the way I did it and he said, 'No, you do it this way, my way'.
Donna:	And you got the same answer?
Claire:	But you get the same answer.
Carol:	He doesn't think he does that. He thinks that he's quite happy for people to do things different ways.
Claire:	He says, 'You do this.' And I say, 'But I don't do that when I'm doing it my way.' He says, 'Yes you do. You do this.' And it just gets into an argument and he ends up yelling at me. So I just don't bother any more. I just go to my mum [or] else I just get the answer out of the back of the book and see how they got it.

The experiences that have influenced students' views can be quite strong and resilient to change. Despite the best intentions of the teacher, students often view the same event in a very different way to that of their teacher. For example, during a project for science, Jeff was particularly impressed by the way James and Robert developed an interesting and inventive idea for testing the viscosity of motor oil. His interpretation of the episode was that James and Robert had hit upon the idea for themselves following a brief discussion in which he raised some problems with their previous idea. Here is James's interpretation.

Carol: What about the idea for doing the test in the first place. How did you get the idea?

James: Oh, we wanted to do oil but we wanted to get the boiling point of it but Mr Northfield said using the Bunsen burner that you couldn't get [enough] heat. Like it [couldn't get] hot [enough] to be able to do it.

Carol: Oil boils at a really high temperature.

James: He didn't tell us but he said we couldn't do it just with a Bunsen burner.

Carol: So how did you get the idea for the viscosity test?

James: Um. Oh, he gave it to us.

Carol: So, did he say to you why don't you test its stickiness?

James: Yeah . . . but when we were planning it he said that could be a way you could do it.

Carol: And then how did you get the idea for how you would test the stickiness?

James: Well he said like you'd need something to drop in so we said a marble or something.

Carol: And was it your idea to heat it up?

James: Yeah. Kind of. Yeah.

This difference in interpretation of the same episode is strikingly apparent when both sides are so explicitly spelt out. However, in the normal rush and bustle of the classroom many other factors also influence events so that they might be misinterpreted; or viewed differently from different perspectives. Students' and teachers' preconceived ideas inevitably influence their interpretation of events.

Fran: Kids understand, like with the fractions I understood what Michelle meant but she didn't understand it so she probably understood me more than teachers.

Michelle: Yeah, teachers . . .

> *Fran:* They're smarter than us and like . . .
>
> *Michelle:* So they expect us to understand what they're saying but we don't.
>
> *Carol:* Do you then say I don't understand that?
>
> *Michelle:* But they don't listen and they think that they [the students] weren't listening.

and

> *Jan:* He listened but he didn't really know what I was talking about.
>
> *Georgia:* I hate it when they don't understand what you're trying to say.
>
> *Jan:* Yeah, like you're trying to say something they don't really know what you're talking about.
>
> *Georgia:* It'd be hard though, you know, to understand.

Perhaps the way students and teachers listen (or do not listen) to each other contributes to this gap in understanding. It is not just words that are heard, there are meanings attached to them and those meanings have already been filtered through the individual's own views of the workplace in which they operate; the school. The language of students and teachers is often different, and this can be a barrier to meaningful communication.

> *Carol:* Is there anything you think teachers could do to help you learn better?
>
> *Janet:* Listen to you more.
>
> *Carol:* Don't you think they do that?
>
> *Janet:* Sometimes they don't.
>
> *Carol:* Do you mean listen to you as a class or listen to you individually?
>
> *Liz:* Well, sometimes when you have trouble individually you can't tell them, you can't explain to them.

and

> When you don't understand something and you go up to the teacher and ask him about it sometimes you can't think of the right words and they just sort of look at you as though you don't know what you're talking about. And it gets really annoying because you just don't know how to explain it. (Rhonda)

Donna suggested one way that she would solve this problem: her ideal way of learning would be to have two teachers in every classroom; one would be the 'helping teacher'. While Claire's teacher would somehow be able to see things from the students' point of view.

> *Donna:* Well, I'd have a teacher that helps the kids. If one teacher was helping someone else, the other teacher would always be there to help someone else.
>
> *Carol:* And what else would you have?
>
> *Claire:* I'd like the teacher to, you know, see things your way.

Teachers are People

Journal: 24th March
A great day — the warm fuzzies in home group were great for everyone including me and everyone went happily into maths for the next lesson.

The home group task which led to this feeling was quite simple. Each student wrote their name at the top of a sheet of paper then passed it on to the student next to them who then wrote a statement about the person whose name appeared at the top of the sheet. After the exchange had begun Jeff and Melissa (another teacher) added their own sheets. The comments made by the students were a reminder that personal qualities are identified and valued as the teaching role is undertaken. The positive comments made about each other allowed participants to leave home group with a sense of worth and the two teachers felt as good as any student in the class.

Perhaps schooling needs to incorporate activities like this more often so that there are more frequent reminders that it is *people* who are occupying the roles of teacher and student, because it seems to us that this point is often overlooked. Consider, for example, Ken who thinks that students are, '. . . just sort of feel like real little people. I'm little and then there's big giants walking around everywhere and you feel nervous'. In order to cope with these feelings, students develop quite clever ways of protecting themselves. Ken and his friend Patrick have definite views about the nature of teachers, the classroom and themselves as students, and they have become quite skilled at operating within these parameters.

Carol:	[Looking at a photograph taken earlier in the year.] There's Patrick there.
Patrick:	Where?
Carol:	Up the back. Do you always sit up the back, Patrick?
Ken:	[Laughs] Yeah.
Patrick:	Especially when I have French.
Carol:	Why do you sit up the back?
Ken:	'Cos it's out of the way and you can do what you like.
Patrick:	When the teachers are looking for people to ask they always go for the third row from the back.
Ken:	I like it because I'm small. Patrick usually sits in front of me and I just duck down low.
Patrick:	And also they always pick me 'cos they can see me.
Carol:	Don't you like being asked?
Patrick:	No. Because I don't know all the questions.
Carol:	What happens if the teacher asks you a question and you don't know the answer?
Patrick:	I say, I just go 'Ummm'.
Ken:	I'd say 'Ummm . . . ummm . . . ummm', and then John usually tells me.

Ken and Patrick have developed a strategy for coping which they have obviously found successful. From a teacher's perspective it is not an approach which will be beneficial in helping them to learn for understanding, but for Ken and Patrick it works to protect them as people from the embarrassment and difficulties of 'not knowing'. These strategies are so important in shaping their views of teaching, learning and the workplace of school. There would need to be some fairly powerful incentives in this workplace to encourage Ken and Patrick to change their well-developed and successful coping strategies. The difficulty in teaching is that here are two individuals in a class of twenty-five that can so easily be treated as a part of a group rather than as important persons with learning needs and concerns. The human impact of schooling is quite complex and it is no wonder that teachers are alarmed at any suggestion that changes in class size would have little impact on teaching and learning.

Students' responses to schooling will be filtered through their lens of existing perceptions and acted on through the coping behaviors they have already adopted. So from a student's perspective, why do teachers ask them to do things in school? because that is what they are paid to do; and why do students usually work through what they are asked to do in a passive and uncritical way? because that is what they think they need to do to cope with their work between clocking on and clocking off: and they do not get paid. However, despite all of this there are still successes which challenge the system. The following extracts from some of the students' reports (see 'Personal Reports', Chapter 5; last week in November, p. 51) about themselves demonstrate many of the points highlighted in this chapter. The reports are indicative of the range of responses Jeff received and demonstrate how this group of students have developed the ability to recognize their own learning behaviors and how these shape their achievements. Considering the views of success that the students suggested in Chapter 10, these reports offer another perspective. It is also interesting to see how similar themes emerge in their responses and how some ideas are 'revisited' by others — sometimes seating arrangements are quite obvious to teachers. At the same time, of course, there are those who demonstrate how their perceptions of themselves are too great to be changed by one teacher in one year.

Write about your progress during the year

Fran: I have been getting most of my work done. I think that I get easily distracted and carried away some-times, but in the past three weeks or so my behavior has changed dramatically. I understand the work we get given but if I don't I ask for help.

Donna: I think I would give my report between A–D be-cause I don't think I've tried very hard cause I've been a bit silly.

Rhonda: I don't know anything.

John: My progress during the year has been good, I have learned many things and I have worked well.

Gayle: I am very OK at maths and science. I think my marks have improved in all of my subjects. I have tried hard and kept my work neat.

Fred: I think I improved heaps this term. My books got neater. I'm very good at the microscopes and I did okay on the time test. But you think I copied John but how could I when I got higher marks — ever thought he copied me?

Claire: On most of my tests I either get a pass or a high mark, I work consistently (most of the time) but can be distracted easily. I make sure that I understand all of my work.

James: I think that I have done well during the year and have stayed the same in the results of tests but I have got better at learning.

What do you need to do to improve your results in the future?

Fran: I need to study more and concentrate more.

Donna: Try harder and think more by not being silly.

Rhonda: Try harder in just about everything.

John: Work a bit harder.

Gayle: I need to improve on my behavior cause sometimes my grades are bad.

Fred: Study harder, and work neater to get extra marks.

Claire: Behave, pay attention, put my best effort into my work, arrive on time and hand things in on time, co-operate, not get distracted easily.

James: Work well at home and keep trying to understand something without going to someone else.

If you get a bad result on a maths test, what are the most likely reasons?

Fran: Probably not studying and not concentrating enough.

Donna: I might copy someone but it might only be one or two questions and I would make up the marks I lost.

Rhonda: Silly mistakes. Not paying attention in class.

John: Stupid little things like not carrying [the number in maths problems] or something like that.

Gayle: I didn't study. Silly slips.

Fred: Because if the girls at the back sit near you then they giggle and whisper and it puts you off and you go blank. Get rid of the girls Fran, Claire, Trish, Linda, Michelle, Jan, Donna and Gayle, because they're trouble-makers.

Claire: That I have had silly mistakes or I haven't paid attention in class. But I always make up for my tests, if I am not pleased by the mark I receive. If I don't make up for the test, I make sure I can understand where I have gone wrong.

James: That I didn't concentrate enough. I didn't work enough and try enough in learning the subject or I was distracted during the test.

If A is excellent and E is a pass, what letter grade do you think you deserve?

Linda: Mathematics — B⁺ because I'm all right at it but I'm not excellent.
Science — B because I'm not very good at it.

Donna: Mathematics — A because I'm all right at it.
Science — B because I'm not very good at it but I try.

Rhonda: Mathematics — D because I am dumb at maths.
Science — C⁻ cause I am nearly as bad at science as I am at maths.

John: Mathematics — A because of my ability, good marks, happy to help.
Science — A⁻ or B⁺ because I contribute to groups well. Accept responsibility.

Gayle: Mathematics — Good at her work, understands work. And if all else failed she likes to catch up.
Science — B⁺ very good at her work and *is capable of doing her work.*

Fred: Mathematics — B⁺ my book is okay and I do okay at my work.
Science — A because my book is neat and has everything it has to have in it e.g., index. And I work good in class.

Claire: Mathematics — A
Science — A

James: Mathematics — A Project and book markings were good. Completes work. Accepts all work with a positive attitude. Can explain things.

Science — A can contribute into class discussion. Completed assignments and tests. Can explain things.

Kathy: Mathematics — B⁺ because at the start I didn't give a very good attitude towards maths because I didn't understand the basics, and my marks weren't good. Science — A because I always try to do things properly and participate in all the experiments. I even won a prize for designing the boat which could carry the most.

Dermot: Mathematics — E because I'm not excellent.
Science — E because I haven't done any homework.

List some of the things you do which makes your learning better

Linda: Maths challenge boxes work.
Science — experiments.

Donna: Work problem boxes in maths.
More experiments in science.

Rhonda: More hands-on things and a trip to Scienceworks (interactive science museum).

John: Concentrating. Write calculations out fully.

Gayle: Maths I study and work hard for tests. Completes homework. Science — works hard in class *most of the time* and completes homework.

Fred: Like when he bought that video in with the diving and we did decimals. Also going outside activities.

James: Able to concentrate. Good teacher. Enjoyable things such as problems in maths and experiments in science.

Kathy: The problems and things in maths we do help me understand maths better and the sheets which explain things in science help me understand.

Dermot: Not talking, listening, no detentions, I would work better without Miss X.

Jan: Stop daydreaming, listen to instructions, if I have nothing around me to play with I concentrate better.

What do you think you need to do to improve your learning in mathematics and science?

Linda: Be more sensible.

Donna: Try a bit harder, try to be a bit more sensible.

Rhonda: Everything.

John: Keep workbook tidier. Follow instructions *properly*.

Gayle: Gayle is *sometimes* disruptive to the class in maths and science. Could improve on behavior.

Fred: I think I need to improve in maths a bit. I would do better if I could choose the teacher I wanted for different subjects. That's all folks.

James: Accept responsibility to help other people.

Kathy: Do more problems in maths and do more experiments in science.

Dermot: Do some more work, don't mess around.

It seems that these students certainly know enough about themselves and their practices to be able to take more responsibility for their learning behavior in school. Perhaps this is a first and important step in encouraging that to occur.

Learning from Experience

This section of the book describes what we consider to be some of the important implications for teaching and teacher education as a result of Jeff's teaching experience. The investment of time and energy so necessary for teaching are intensely personal, yet by reviewing the experiences at the end of the school year the bigger picture slowly emerges. The importance of reflection on practice is abundantly clear throughout this section and highlights the need for each teacher's pedagogical knowledge to be much better recognized and valued. This section is our attempt to share the experience more widely and invite teachers and others to consider our findings with their experience. One of the teacher reviewers commented, '. . . there is a shock of recognition . . . which is true for many teachers . . . it is a shame teachers do so much in isolation.' This is our attempt to show the complexity of teaching in a way that may be recognized.

Chapter 11

Implications for Teaching and Learning

Overview

This section begins with an outline of what we consider to be some of the implications for teaching and learning that we have distilled from Jeff's reflection on his experience. These implications are organized in this chapter using a thematic approach comprising five major headings: nature of learning; creating conditions for learning; student perspectives on learning; process of teaching and learning; and, overall reactions.

Assessing the Effort

It seems inevitable that the nature of teaching causes teachers to rarely be satisfied with their students' learning outcomes. They see so much of the individual's potential and ability and always strive to see that these be fully attained. Some students will make good progress, others will not capitalize on the possibilities offered to them. Through Jeff's teaching experience we have learnt that his priorities for learning were not always widely shared amongst the students. However, considering what we now understand about the events and episodes, it does seem as though the students' responses to the learning demands were reasonable given their perspectives and experience. The opportunity to appreciate the students' perspectives through Carol's interaction with the students has been invaluable in helping us understand the classroom events from different perspectives.

From a teacher perspective, the inability to consistently create and manage the conditions which could encourage more active independent learning was frustrating. The dailiness of teaching and the management priorities may have been anticipated, but over time it is difficult for one to accept the fact that it is an extremely difficult task to teach in ways that match the learning goals and aspirations that Jeff brought with him to this teaching experience. In this respect, Jeff may describe himself as a 'living contradiction' (Whitehead, 1993) with values, beliefs and aspirations that are difficult to translate into practice. However, we would argue that a very important facet of this experience is not that the teaching and learning hopes and goals were not fully attained, but that the struggle to reach them was continual, consistent and purposeful. It is this effort and persistence that we see as important as it is an example of the possibilities that become available when one teaches 'against the grain' (Cochran-Smith, 1991). But successes did occur:

Journal, 6th May
A routine day which finished with a highlight at the end of the last period. Maths very routine checking homework and 're-deeming' test errors. No problems but disappointed with students' limited organisational skills. Teaching reminds you of the little things, forgotten homework, forgotten books, that need to be handled as you try to develop conditions and opportunities for learning.

The science class followed as we continued with the full and empty coffee jars rolling and dropped from a height. We checked our observation of the dropping jars and then discussed our explanations of our observations. Students then wrote their own responses. When I asked how many students now felt they wanted 'answers' from me I was pleased to hear the students did not feel this was appropriate. When I asked why, they readily responded that 'We have to understand'. 'It would not matter what you said, it is what we think that matters.' This wide rejection of the 'right answer' being provided was encouraging. They certainly saw a mismatch between the POE approach and giving a right answer. Another time when I wished I had taped the episode or there had been an outsider to discuss the student response. With the daily routine things are happening — I wouldn't have believed it if I had not heard it.

For Jeff, the outcome of this classroom activity remains a highlight from the year. The activity was structured so that students would *predict* what would happen (which coffee jar will roll further on the ground after being released on a slope: the jar filled with sand or the empty jar?). Then they *observed* what did happen; in this case observing the jars rolling down a slope in the school quadrangle. The students completed the POE activity by *explaining* the observation. In this case the explanation had extended for 15 minutes with most students involved and Jeff expressed satisfaction with their explanations. His automatic teacher response was to conclude the discussion and provide a more 'scientific' explanation. The class felt this was not needed, 'It would not matter what you said, it is what we think that matters.' Quite a rewarding experience indeed.

At the time this was interpreted as students accepting responsibility for their own learning and assessing their level of understanding; a breakthrough. Yet if this was the case, why did it not continue in this vein and happen more often? Why was change so slow? Perhaps the tension between Jeff's and the students' differing expectations of learning meant that change could be nothing other than slow and painful. The students certainly had good reason to be wary of the changes being imposed. They had years of experience which taught them that this learning for understanding was not always necessary, nor always rewarded in school. Maybe every now and again their resistance was lowered as they gained some tacit rewards from their learning which buoyed them sufficiently to see the point of an activity; and accept its value.

At the end of the year, Jeff reviewed all of the data and experiences and identified and developed a number of themes. Each theme emerged by reflecting on particular events and anecdotes (both as independent and interdependent episodes) and reframing the situations to learn from these experiences. With the wisdom of his classroom practice and the rush and bustle of daily school life behind him, he was able to apply his skills as an educational researcher to the 'data'. With his recent and considerable classroom experience underpinning his views, he developed summary statements of the teaching and learning issues. These themes (see Table 1) form a framework which we will use to discuss the findings which have emerged from a very significant personal learning experience.

The Nature of Learning

Jeff attempted to change the students' perception of the role of the teacher as well as their perception of their role in learning. He found that with learner consent the teacher-dependent student who was a passive recipient of knowledge and an uncritical thinker could be altered to one who was an active, independent and purposeful constructor of knowledge who could be involved in quality learning experiences. But this would be uncommon in situations where the learning was done *to* the student rather than *by* the student.

Throughout the years of schooling, students develop their own

Table 1: Learning from a teaching experience

Nature of Learning
1   Quality learning requires learner consent.
2   Learning is done *by* rather than *to* students.
3   Student prior experiences are crucial and often do not fit the learning demands expected.
4   Effort and risk taking are critical for learning.
5   Understanding is rarely experienced, and not expected, by many students.

Creating Conditions for Learning
6   Teacher change precedes student change.
7   Changes in assessment (beliefs and practice) are essential. Students must see ideas and activities which improve the learning being valued.
8   Self-confidence and trust are critical attributes for students.
9   There is a need to have a balance between management demands and maintaining learning opportunities in the classroom.
10 Students can have a significant impact on classroom climate. It only takes a few students to make a big difference.
11 There is a limit to the thinking and learning demands that can be placed on students.
12 There is a need for teachers to respond to contextual factors and make intuitive decisions rather than always following the plan.

Student Perspectives on Learning
13 Success is gained by the 'right answers' to defined tasks.
14 Enjoyment is regarded with suspicion in terms of learning.
15 Lessons with different teachers allow a 'fresh start' and give students a chance to see their tasks as being well defined.
16 Students have faith in texts: the tasks are routine and the knowledge is dependable.
17 Students wish to be successful but to be seen as 'mediocre' by their peers.

Process of Teaching and Learning
18 Effective interventions increase the spread of students.
19 Frequent use of particular teaching strategies leads to passive student responses.
20 It is important to increase the repertoire of teaching strategies.
21 In the 'dailiness' of schooling there are still rare opportunities for active learning.

Overall Reactions
22 Time and careful review are essential for professional development.
23 It is important to have a model and language of learning so that students and teachers can discuss teaching and learning issues.
24 Understanding student responses requires details of student and class context (social structures, expectations of other teachers, etc.).

---

views about what to expect from certain situations. They learn how to act and respond to a variety of stimuli. Their responses are not always in the form of behaviors which will assist them in their learning, but they commonly help them to cope with the 'routine' demands of school. Therefore, their prior experiences are crucial in shaping their learning behavior and, sadly, often do not fit the learning demands expected. This is particularly highlighted when the learning demands require students to make an effort and to take risks to further their understanding. However, these are behaviors, which in themselves are critical for learning, but can be difficult to encourage in students who do not have the confidence to take the 'leap of faith' necessary to push the boundaries in their learning. As a result of the accumulation of experiences that do not actively encourage quality learning, it is not uncommon for students to rarely experience genuine understanding of the content being taught, hence they do not tend to link understanding with learning, so they do not expect to learn with understanding. All they need is to 'know' the work.

The idea that learning requires learner consent then is obvious, but it is most difficult to achieve. It clearly requires independence on the part of the student and there are many features of classrooms that make this difficult to achieve for individuals. Twenty-five students have to be managed and students have learned that this management role is very important for teaching. The peer group requires a degree of conforming if students are to 'fit in', so the risk-taking associated with independence is going to take some self-confidence and support from peers. A key factor may be the stability of the immediate peer group. For some students the feeling that the support of immediate friends will remain seems to be important in their willingness to consent to think and offer their ideas.

Jeff felt that the class was easy to teach in that they were willing to engage in defined tasks and what could be called busy work. When required to make decisions and think and work independently common responses included,

We may be wrong.

You know the answers . . . why don't you just tell us.

You are the teacher . . . you should tell us.

The Velcro activity (see Chapter 6) led to this form of response. In this case the possible value of reading carefully and thinking about the meaning and creating possible sub-headings and headings for the information was not acknowledged. More structured activities such as the mathematics problem tasks and electric circuit boards were more successful because the feedback was more immediate. Students need to learn to see the value of their independence perhaps by having structured (and successful) experiences. Perhaps the age and social development of these Year 7 students made it difficult for many of them to take an independent approach and consent to individual learning. The risks were too great and it only required a small number of students to raise doubts about the value of some activities for this to begin to impact on the learning experience.

Jeff began by looking for the right conditions to introduce activities that would have high impact. The value of independent thinking would be self-evident for students. Hindsight would suggest that a more consistent use of structured activities that provided feedback for students would have been a more effective approach. The attempt to gain student consent to work and think independently remained part of Jeff's agenda but there was little evidence of wide and consistent student acceptance.

Doing what is expected and working hard are the predominant values. They have not seen the value of independent thinking and this is rarely valued in the way students are assessed. The students are in mid-career in their schooling. They are responding to what is needed to complete this phase of their lives. Risk-taking and thinking are not yet associated with assisting their progress in school. The difficulty for Jeff was in learning how to more effectively convince students that their consent to learn (required for thinking and understanding) was a valuable asset for their negotiation of the demands of schooling.

The conditions for learning all follow from the above considerations. What is needed if active independent learning is to be valued by students?

Creating Conditions for Learning

Although the themes within the nature of learning may appear intelligible (that they make sense and can be understood) and plausible (that they seem reasonable to do), any attempt to make them fruitful for the learner (be worth the effort) will revolve around the conditions for learning which are necessary to encourage the changes in learning behaviors. Therefore the notion of intelligible, plausible and fruitful (Posner *et al.*, 1982; Hewson; 1982) takes on new significance because being able to create the conditions for learning are imperative if fruitfulness is to lead students to the rewards they require to pursue learning in a more active manner — more often.

To create the conditions for learning, teachers need to recognize and understand that teacher change precedes student change. Change in this case refers to the expectations, practices and beliefs that underpin their pedagogy. For teacher change of this nature to occur, it is essential that they be associated with changes in assessment beliefs and practices so that students see that the ideas and activities that improve learning are valued.

Self-confidence and trust are critical attributes for students and are also essential constituents in the conditions for learning. As Section 1 of this book demonstrates, a constant effort on the teacher's part to encourage students to have trust in themselves and their classroom environment is critical to encourage more independent learning. Developing students' confidence and trust is a continual process and one that should not too readily be taken for granted.

The balancing of management with teaching and learning demands was always difficult. The requirement to provide teaching and learning activities that captured interest meant being very sensitive to the class climate. Determining readiness for particular tasks was difficult. In some cases, the continual need to manage the class and the teacher's responses associated with this need can be quite incompatible with the expectation of accepting more responsibility for learning. In essence then, the teacher's responses to one concern (classroom management) may inadvertently undermine the teacher's concerns to encourage particular learning responses. Similarly, individual students have the power to shape the classroom climate. It only takes a few students to make a big difference to the mood and behavior within the class. The teacher alone is not the sole factor influencing (or controlling) the classroom climate. It could well be argued that although the class largely contains the same group of students, that in fact the class is actually never really 'the same'. In some ways there is really no such thing as the 'normal class' as individual moods, feelings and emotions can make such a difference to the nature of the class.

Some of the elements that contribute to the conditions of learning are in dynamic equilibrium for much of the time as the teacher skilfully manages a number of often conflicting issues and concerns. However, one that is by no means easy to gauge is associated with the degree of difficulty students may perceive a learning task to contain. Apparently straightforward tasks may be demanding or cause anxiety for students especially if an activity is new or there is confusion about the outcomes expected. There is certainly a limit to the thinking and learning demands that can be placed on students. Ascertaining these limits is difficult for the teacher as they fluctuate with, for example, the type of task, the subject matter, the classroom climate, and students' confidence. Also, thinking is a demanding activity and believing that students can (or should) be thinking all day is unreasonable. With each change of lesson, new demands and expectations are placed on the students and they may not be capable of quality thinking throughout all of these experiences. Therefore, recognizing and choosing the 'right time' for activities can be a difficult and frustrating experience. Perhaps that is why it is so important for teachers to be able to respond to contextual factors and make intuitive decisions rather than always following their plan.

The ability to respond to contextual factors is related to the teacher's experience and an understanding that one can afford to listen to the students and react accordingly. As a class unfolds, being able to respond to the contextual factors may be akin to seeing the plan for the lesson as only one amongst an array of competing alternatives. This is perhaps where the teacher's craft knowledge (Grimmett and MacKinnon, 1992) is being developed, it is highlighted through reflection-in-action. It also, demonstrates that the 'when' of reflection (Loughran, 1996) influences the learning about teaching. Responding to contextual factors is then when the true tact of teaching (van Manen, 1991a) is being fully demonstrated as the listening encourages a greater sense of understanding the situation.

Students' Perspectives on Learning

The discussion in this section tends to affirm and articulate that which many experienced teachers carry as tacit knowledge. For Jeff, the consistent approach to maintaining a journal helped articulate this tacit knowledge. What became obvious to him emerged as a result of the time and effort put into reflecting on the issues. The research knowledge that helped him to organize and understand the principles of his teaching did not necessarily assist him in the rush and bustle of actual classroom practice. Yet each individual anecdote or episode provided a focus for increasing overall understanding. In a similar way the use of cases (Shulman, 1992; Shulman and Mesa-Bains, 1993) highlights teacher responses to particular events and invites the reader to make links with similar experiences and build a deeper understanding of teaching and learning. This section therefore demonstrates how when re-reading his journal, and reconsidering the events it described, Jeff was prompted to reconsider (after the event) his understanding of his overall experiences as a teacher.

Despite the teacher's intentions, from a student's perspective success is gained by the 'right answers' to defined tasks. In one sense, the greater the certainty associated with the task, the easier (and safer) it is for students to pursue success as they know what they are aiming for. It is interesting to note that when learning tasks move away from being clear and rigid, students begin to become suspicious of change. This can happen when the tasks involve enjoyment. Paradoxically, the introduction of interest and enjoyment in learning can be a signal to students that the demands are changing and that they should be 'on their guard'. The students themselves also have signs that learning is different. Although they may be enjoying their experiences, the lack of 'acceptable' measures of school work (taking notes, use of text book, etc.) for them may mean that the work is less valuable, or that there is 'too much thinking and not enough work'. Enjoyment and a move away from the 'routine' may not be equated with work, because work has a record of the activity, and the learning can be clearly seen by students.

The certainty of knowing the 'routine' brings with it certain advantages. The secondary school structure, which generally leads to subjects being taught by different teachers, is an important aspect of learning because it allows a 'fresh start'. These 'fresh starts' are reassuring for students as they give them a chance to see their tasks as being well defined; there is comfort in knowing the structure. The advantages of reassurance through structure is perhaps never so clear as it is through the faith students have in texts. For them the tasks are routine and the knowledge is dependable and they can generally function comfortably in the knowledge of knowing about the 'routine'. Therefore, documenting evidence of doing work (e.g., notes) is important to the students regardless of whether they actually learn from doing the work. Learning may be regarded as something very different to work and understanding is generally not a part of school learning.

One of the most powerful influences on students' views of learning is their peer group and their position in it. Strangely, although students wish to be successful they generally prefer to be seen as 'mediocre' by their peers. Standing out as being different or 'better' than the others in the peer group is not a helpful way of being perceived. Therefore, in everyday student interaction, being the same as everyone else is important. This is indeed interesting because as individuals they wish to be successful: they just do not want to be seen as different.

For the teacher, there is a real dilemma. Publicly congratulating a student for good learning could be unwanted praise for the student. The student could be seen as being set apart from the peer group and therefore attract unwanted attention from colleagues. Public recognition for some students could then be hindering the shift in learning behaviors that a teacher is trying to encourage. The teacher's ability to recognize and respond appropriately to individuals is then very important. Students appreciate private affirmation but may be embarrassed if this occurs publicly.

This is, however, influenced by the type of activity. For structured, standard, defined, routine tasks, where the emphasis is on completing 'the work', public acknowledgment may well be acceptable. It is when the work involves learning which highlights individual differences that tensions may arise. From Jeff's perspective, James was the only student in 7D who was comfortable with being seen as a good learner among his peers. He was happy with his own self-image and was not influenced by the peer group when it came to standing out as different (see Chapter 9, pp. 99–101: What does it mean to be successful?)

The Process of Teaching and Learning

One of the most telling outcomes of Jeff's teaching was associated with the impact of his teaching strategies. As he worked to introduce teaching strategies that would encourage the students to be more active in their learning, it became clear on a number of occasions that the effective interventions increased the spread of students. Although the activities themselves were successful, one consequence was that the ability of the teacher to monitor 'where each student was' with respect to learning became more difficult and led to increased demands. Thus, the students who were most able and confident appeared to benefit most from the change in activities. However, this is not to suggest that others did not also benefit. In fact the advantages for all students were obvious at different times, but the gains in learning were not uniform for all members of the class. In some ways, the more successful a teaching strategy was, the more of a potential problem it created. In one approach to completing maths problems, Jeff initiated a move whereby students could demonstrate to him when they understood the task by completing the example problem kept at the front of the class. Clearly, some students could do this quickly and others could not. This strategy was a response to a reasonable argument put forward by some students that they had little need to complete many problems after they had already gained a mastery of the task. However, some students struggled to gain a competency with the task despite extensive practice. The change was successful but created a need for strategies that would extend the capable and confident students while allowing longer support for the slower, less confident students.

Clearly then, it is important for teachers to increase the repertoire of teaching strategies at their disposal so that their choice of pedagogy is appropriately aligned with the learning styles they hope to develop. But, almost regardless of the strategies, frequent use of particular teaching strategies leads to passive student responses. It is curious that 'chalk and talk' is such a dominant form of teaching when most teachers immediately recognize the passive student responses it invokes. Yet most are prepared to accept it because they believe it to be the most time efficient and effective method for managing the class group and transferring information; the irony is that the same cannot be said for the resultant student learning. Another aspect of this point is that the teaching strategy alone is not necessarily the 'active' constituent of the task, it is the learning that is active as a result of appropriate use of the strategy. This is one reason why teachers need a range of teaching strategies. Teaching strategies need to be used with purpose and so it is the desired learning outcomes that should help to direct the pedagogy employed.

Students have strategies for coping and responding to the classroom demands set for them (see Chapters 8 and 9). There is a 'dailiness' to schooling, as in any workplace, whereby the routines and structures encourage passivity and acceptance of the commonplace. However, even in this dailiness there are still rare opportunities for active learning. These opportunities may sometimes be grasped by the students when the conditions for learning and their perspective of a task or activity are challenged, but generally it would appear to us that these opportunities are better recognized and grasped when the teacher is responsive to the pedagogical moment (van Manen, 1991b). Listening to the students, attempting to balance the teacher's agenda with the students' needs and perceptions, and being aware of the complex nature of the classroom moment by moment is demanding, yet within all of this, the skilled pedagogue is still capable of recognizing opportunities for learning, and is able to grasp them.

Overall Reactions

As an experienced teacher educator, Jeff sought the teaching allotment for 7D. His hopes and aspirations were based on a well-formed and articulated belief, and teaching and learning, system; something that many teachers have not had the opportunity or time to develop themselves. Therefore, what for many teachers maybe tacit knowledge, was more explicit for Jeff. But even with this important feature of understanding about teaching and learning he still recognized that for his ongoing professional development, time and careful review were essential. The teaching experience certainly challenged his ideas and beliefs, and some of these were probably quite shaken at different times, but he noted the value and importance of having a model and language of learning. This is an important element of a teacher's professional knowledge for it allows them to discuss, and therefore better understand, teaching and learning issues; with both their colleagues and — something which can be too easily overlooked — their students. In fact the need to develop a vocabulary of learning with students is an area of development that Macdonald (1996) has demonstrated as being particularly valuable for enhancing responsibility for learning. Jeff explored the use of a vocabulary for learning with 7D (see Good Learning Behaviors, Chapter 9, pp. 96–8) and attempted to help them better identify their approach to learning. Clearly, the use of a model could help students to better 'link', 'understand' and 'think' about their own learning.

Despite all of this, there is no doubt that understanding students and their responses to teaching, learning and schooling, requires details about the individuals and class context (social structures, expectations of other teachers, etc.), something which is time and energy consuming, and essential for fostering and managing a learning environment. Much of what happens in a class may be embedded in events which is not immediately obvious to the teacher, and the context then affects the classroom climate. In some cases there may be a need to look well outside the classroom and its experiences to understand what is really happening and why (refer to the Goody Goody Class, Chapter 7, pp. 72–5).

Learning from and through experience is then paramount to the development of teachers and is not something that can ever be taken for granted. Interpersonal skills and relationships are central to the communication of quality teaching and learning. Through sharing some of the insights of the episodes that Jeff experienced while teaching 7D, we hope that they help communicate to others some of these important facets of the complexity of teaching, learning and schooling.

Chapter 12

Some Final Reflections

Overview

Learning from and through experience has been an important aspect of this book. We close by reflecting on the total experience and attempting to place some of this learning in a context that demonstrates the difficulties of attempting to revisit secondary school teaching and to portray this event in a meaningful way for others. It is therefore a personal reflection on what was an important opportunity and experience.

Reviewing the Purpose of the Book

In recent times, educational literature has shown a move towards incorporating the teacher's voice as a way of better acknowledging the importance of teachers' views in, and descriptions of, episodes and events. This trend is also respecting teachers' knowledge and experience (Britzman, 1991; Carter, 1993) in ways which were not common only a decade ago. The manner in which we have presented the first eleven chapters of this book has been an attempt to place the teacher (Jeff) at the centre of the experience and to give the context that is so important in supporting the knowledge that is derived from listening to the teacher's voice. We believe that in so doing, Hargreaves' (1996) concern that the 'teacher's voice' be presented critically and contextually begins to be addressed. The book is therefore an attempt to develop our understanding of teaching and learning by studying an extensive teaching experience from three perspectives: teacher, learner, researcher. Through Carol's involvement we have also been able to incorporate the 'students' voice' in ways that we trust is faithful to their concerns and intentions.

With this in mind, we close this book with a personal reflection that in many ways bridges the dichotomy that Fenstermacher (1994) alludes to as he distinguishes between, '. . . the knowledge that teachers generate as a result of their experience as teachers, in contrast to the knowledge of teaching that is generated by those who specialise in research on teaching' (p. 3). Yet as this book has developed we have not overtly distinguished between either; rather we have attempted to understand the teaching and learning that Jeff was involved in and to try to portray that in ways that would be identifiable and understandable to others. Hence we believe that this also demonstrates an important aspect of self-study. Valuable learning occurs when self-study is a shared task. As Jeff explains in the next section, it may well be that although the learning is intensely personal, self-study itself requires collaboration and this book is an example of such collaboration; 'a shared adventure' (Loughran and Gunstone, 1996).

Jeff's Reflections

For many years I have pondered the way in which teacher knowledge and experience has been regarded by teachers and other educationalists. I have repeatedly heard comments such as, 'I am only a teacher' when teachers introduce themselves at the start of a new course; 'It is only about me and my teaching' when sharing their experiences, and; 'It is only in my classroom in my school' that indicates that teachers feel their knowledge and experience does not extend beyond their own situation. I find myself thinking the same way about the story of my experiences in the secondary classroom as documented through this book. Educationalists like Tom Russell have observed how many teachers have learned to rely on educational ideas coming from outside the profession. Policy and curriculum ideas have generally been produced by others, with teachers the first targets of the change process. Teacher ability to adapt ideas to suit particular contexts have been part of the rhetoric but it has been rare to have the introduction of new ideas associated with the time and support needed for teachers to implement new approaches with understanding. Teacher personal opinions have had little place in the introduction of most educational change. Teacher knowledge and experience is rarely regarded as a sound basis for shaping educational change. Teacher knowledge has been regarded as idiosyncratic and difficult to analyse and be understood in any generalizable way.

While teachers may acknowledge external knowledge as having higher status than their own knowledge, they are quick to point out that educational theories and ideas are often irrelevant in assisting them to address day-to-day teaching concerns. After returning to school teaching I can identify closely with the teacher feelings about the educational knowledge that matters. From the perspective of an educational researcher I had to come to terms with the teacher knowledge I was gaining. It was extremely powerful but closely linked to a particular class of students in particular contexts. It was difficult to analyse and communicate to others. My day-to-day concerns did not seem to fit with the diverse range of ideas and theories I had in my background. Teaching made me feel that my growing knowledge was limited, like the teachers who made the comments at the start of this section. Yet I had begun the teaching experience encouraged by teachers who had communicated their efforts to transform their classrooms. They had seemed to make new learning possibilities achievable, providing teaching strategies and evidence of more exciting teaching and learning.

For me, the return to teaching was often a confusing and unsettling experience. The conditions rarely seemed to be suitable to initiate different teaching-learning activities with the class. My journal entries continued to outline disappointments as I searched for understanding of my context. The dailiness of teaching and its unpredictability appeared to dominate my reflections. As I began to understand the student perspective, their responses to the demands of their schooling often made more sense than the learning attitudes and outcomes I was seeking. Yet the overall experience with the class was enjoyable and satisfying. What tended to get documented in the journal and discussed with others were the surprises, dilemmas and tensions giving a more negative picture of the experience. Perhaps no teacher is ever completely satisfied with their students' learning outcomes.

My attempt to analyse and communicate my understanding of teaching and learning at the end of the year was only partly successful. I was able to identify the themes discussed in Chapter 11. Very vivid and significant teaching episodes should have been a basis for understanding but it was difficult to separate my own responses and the missed opportunities from any coherent description of progress. For me, the records of the year's teaching formed a disjointed account of teaching and learning. John (Loughran) was able to examine the records without the personal involvement of teaching in this classroom. His analysis now allows me a clearer understanding of my teaching and learning experience and the nature of teacher knowledge and its generation.

On reflection, my frustration during the year was in trying to analyse the day-to-day teaching experiences in a way that might lead to consistent improvement in classroom interactions. I was also struggling to find ways of communicating my 'teacher knowledge'. I was experiencing the earlier observations made about teachers and their knowledge, yet feeling that I should have been able to better understand and use my experience. I would argue that teacher knowledge has different characteristics in the way it is developed and used. In this chapter I will develop this theme and several other insights that emerge from John's analysis. The first insight comes from an analysis of a perspective that forms a theme throughout the previous chapters — students see their schooling experience in different ways to the intended purposes for many of our classroom activities.

Contrasting Views of Teaching and Learning

Carol Jones provided a way of obtaining a student perspective on the classroom experiences. Her visits to the class on one day each week allowed her to be accepted by the students. She was able to participate in the activities in the morning and then talk with students about what had happened and about their overall views of schooling. She was able to present a student perspective which focused on their ways of coping with schooling. 'Many students see themselves as in the middle of their first work experience.' They know they are required to participate in about twelve years of formal schooling and their previous experiences have allowed them to form views of what is valued and how to best cope with the expectations of their parents and friends. Schooling is also closely associated with personal and social development challenges for young people. Not surprisingly, the establishment of personal identity and relationships dominate the concerns and priorities of young people, aged 11–13 years, in the school setting.

These student perspectives on schooling allowed the student responses to teaching and learning situations to be interpreted with some understanding. At times I was able to introduce classroom activities intended to encourage more active learning among students. Finding appropriate contexts for such activities was not easy and the journal accounts deal with the frustration of the dailiness of teaching. The opportunities to present activities such as Predict Observe Explain (POE), Concept Maps, Inserting titles and sub-headings etc., were based on a view of teaching and learning which could be expressed as in Table 2.

It was difficult to reflect the views of teaching and learning outlined in Table 2 in any sustained way but the six points give some indication of my hopes for the students and their learning experiences. It focuses on students as learners but largely ignores the personal development and relationship priorities of the young people and their past experience of schooling and the way they might manage the demands of schools. Carol was able to present a student perspective on our classroom setting as a result of her extensive discussions with students (see Table 3).

Table 2: *A personal view of teaching and learning*

- Where possible students should have opportunities to be active and think about their learning experiences.
- Students should experience success in learning and gain the confidence and skills to become better learners.
- Linking experiences from both within and outside school greatly assists learning.
- Effort and involvement are important outcomes of school activities and students need to gain credit and encouragement for their efforts.
- Enjoyment and satisfaction with learning are important outcomes.
- Learning involving the above features requires learner consent.

Table 3: *Some student views of teaching and learning*

- Learning is associated with gaining right answers and thinking and personal understanding are just different and often frustrating ways of achieving the required outcomes.
- The learning process and thinking is difficult to associate with school work, and texts and notes are important indicators that school learning is occurring.
- Linking experiences is very demanding and unreasonable when added to the classroom demands for students.
- The final grade is the critical outcome and the basis by which progress is judged.
- Enjoyment is not always associated with school learning — real learning is hard and not usually enjoyed.
- Learning is done to students and teachers have a major responsibility for achieving learning.

The student perspective provides some explanation for student reservations about one teacher taking them for extended periods of time, their reluctance to become involved in more open-ended learning tasks, their dominant concerns for their image among their peers, and the importance of final assessment grades as indications of learning progress.

My initial aspirations for learning lacked any appreciation of the school and classroom context. The value of active learning, thinking and understanding is not self-evident for students and I had greatly under-estimated what was needed for my agenda to be appreciated by students. I was disappointed that I could not become the teacher I had hoped. Management of the group sometimes became my dominant concern, and this too often led to routine teaching and few opportunities for active learning activities.

The successes in learning appeared to arise in unpredictable ways. Planned activities often failed — students were not ready and I tried to by-pass contextual factors. As I learned to listen to students I became better at capitalizing on opportunities. My ideas and experience became better connected to the individuals and their concerns, interests and abilities. What does this mean for teacher education?

Implications for Teacher Education

As a person who had spent more than twenty years in teacher education, the teaching experience was disappointing in a number of respects:

- My wide understanding of educational theories did not seem to assist me in interpreting many of the situations which arose in the classroom. There seemed to be few guidelines for future actions. Perhaps I was preoccupied with a few areas of concern and overlooked situations where my background and experience led to clear responses. In the end, the unique classroom situations require unique and creative responses by teachers which are based on many considerations including background educational knowledge.

- My successes in encouraging quality learning came largely from unplanned opportunities when I listened to students and had the confidence and experience to respond at the time. Much of teacher education is developed and presented external to the school setting. At pre-service level, lectures and seminars are provided to hopefully link with periods of school experience. The importance of lesson planning is taken for granted yet my experience suggested that *my* 'lesson plans' indicated *my* agenda and there were times when I should have listened to students as a source of learning opportunities. Perhaps lesson planning is critical, especially as less experienced teachers build a wider repertoire and learn to interpret student responses. But how can we develop a teacher education approach that encourages teachers to listen to students, respond confidently and respect the 'authority of their own experience'? (Munby and Russell, 1994). One answer must be to incorporate the school experience into teacher education in more fundamental ways. Contemporary school experience must be the subject of study in teacher education at all levels. School-based teacher education at pre-service level allows new teachers to experience the full range of teaching roles and also makes their experiences the subject of study. Personal theories can be outcomes which can be further studied and linked with more established educational theories as their need and relevance becomes clearer. At the inservice level, current teacher experience can become the subject of study via vignettes and case studies. In this way teacher education can become a more genuine learning about teaching rather than always driven by the external demands of new curriculum and procedures.

- My teaching experiences were not shared with others in any sustained way during the year. The journal documented matters of concern at the end of each day but, as with other teachers, the opportunities to consider them were limited. The next day brings new teaching demands and coping from day to day forms a routine with little opportunity to build on experience and consider events and gain support and ideas from others. The arrival of Carol later in the year and now the opportunity to respond to a colleague's analysis of the records of the experience mean that some study of teaching is possible. Learning about teaching cannot be conducted alone. I had thought I had a well-considered view of teaching and learning and a wide range of teaching activities to achieve quality outcomes. My beliefs and ideas were well developed, but the teaching skills needed to support these aspirations were not developed. My teaching approach was developed in the 1960s and 1970s and did not match my 1980s and 1990s beliefs about teaching and learning. I had also underestimated the importance of studying the school and classroom contexts, and, from their perspective, the students' behavior was very purposeful and reasonable. After a year it was clear that my purposes for achieving more active learning needed to be demonstrated in a more convincing way if students were to value the outcomes as part of their schooling demands.

- The daily experience of teaching was important. The counselling and welfare demands of schooling are only obvious to those working in a school. The management demands of twenty-five or more students in a class should be experienced regularly by those involved in teacher education. The student perspective on schooling and learning is rarely considered in the wider education literature but it is essential if teachers are to interpret student behavior in their classrooms.

The daily experience of teaching forced me to consider the nature of teacher knowledge more carefully. At the end of the year I was able to review the data I had gathered and develop the themes that form Table 1 of Chapter 11 (p. 124). John has been able to analyse the information and identify trends and themes that become apparent to a person not directly involved in the day-to-day teaching. In these ways we were carrying out a traditional research role — analysing data about a teaching experience. However, my time in teaching allowed me to experience the types of tacit knowledge that teachers can develop as part of their teaching role. It is a different form of knowledge, generated in different ways and rarely made more explicit and disseminated beyond individual teachers. It is not highly regarded, even by teachers, because it is seen as very context specific and not generalizable, yet when it is made more explicit in teacher stories and cases it has a significant impact on other teachers and those interested in teaching and learning.

Teacher knowledge in this form is certainly personal and unique to particular classroom contexts. The lack of progress and sense of failure that is represented in what is considered and documented means that it would take confidence and colleague support to share such stories. Any deeper consideration of a particular classroom situation becomes difficult as the teacher needs to respond in the next lesson with the class and live with the consequences of any actions taken. The teacher knowledge remains tacit, with the teacher stories a possible way of communicating significant incidents to connect with related experiences of other teachers. Such stories may affirm other teachers' efforts and provide ideas and deeper understanding for teacher readers.

My journal was therefore a series of personally important incidents and some associated reflections. Each day's reflections were crowded out with the subsequent day's experiences needing thought and attention. John's review allows the incidents to be reconsidered. They can be seen as incidents that can be shared and linked — an example of how teachers can reflect on their own classrooms and study their own teaching.

Teacher knowledge generation (teacher research) depends on teachers finding ways of sharing critical experiences. The tacit experiences must be made explicit if we are to consider alternative frames of reference that may lead to deeper understanding of teaching and learning. The danger is that teachers will interpret situations in ways that reinforce existing perceptions. Genuine study of classrooms is associated with a willingness to reconsider alternative frames of reference and colleagues are an important source of ideas and support as the teaching is reviewed.

Bibliography

BAIRD, J.R. and MITCHELL, I.J. (1986) 'Improving the quality of teaching and learning: An Australian case study — the PEEL project', Melbourne, Monash Printing Services.

BAIRD, J.R. and NORTHFIELD, J.R. (1992) 'Learning from the PEEL experience', Melbourne, Monash Printing Services.

BRITZMAN, D.P. (1991) *Practice Makes Practice: A Critical Study of Learning to Teach*, Albany, State University of New York Press.

CARTER, K. (1993) 'The place of story in the study of teaching and teacher education', *Educational Researcher*, **22**, 1, pp. 5–12.

COCHRAN-SMITH, M. (1991) 'Learning to teach against the grain', *Harvard Educational Review*, **61**, 3, pp. 279–310.

FENSTERMACHER, G.D. (1994) 'The knower and the known: The nature of knowledge in research on teaching', *Review of Research in Education*, **20**, pp. 3–56.

GORDON, S. (1992) 'Paradigms, transitions and the new supervision', *Journal of Curriculum and Supervision*, **8**, 1, pp. 62–76.

GRIMMETT, P.P. and MACKINNON, A.M. (1992) 'Craft knowledge and the education of teachers', *Review of Research in Education*, **18**, pp. 385–456.

HALL, G.E. and HORD, S.M. (1987) *Change in Schools: Facilitating the Process*, New York, State University of New York Press.

HARGREAVES, A. (1996) 'Revisiting voice', *Educational Researcher*, **25**, 1, pp. 12–19.

HEWSON, P.W. (1982) 'A case study of conceptual change in special relativity: The influence of prior knowledge in learning', *European Journal of Science Education*, **4**, 1, pp. 61–78.

LOUGHRAN, J.J. (1996) *Developing Reflective Practice: Learning about Teaching and Learning through Modelling*, London, Falmer Press.

LOUGHRAN, J.J. and GUNSTONE, R.F. (1996) Self-study of teaching and research. A paper presented at the annual meeting of the American Educational Research Association, New York, April, 1996.

MACDONALD, I.H. (1996) Enhancing learning by informed student decision making on learning strategy use. Unpublished Doctoral Thesis, Melbourne, Australia, Monash University.

MUNBY, H. and RUSSELL, T. (1994) 'The authority of experience in learning to teach: Messages from a physics method class,' *Journal of Teacher Education*, **45**, 2, pp. 86–95.

POSNER, G.J., STRIKE, K.A., HEWSON, P.W. and GERTZOG, W.A. (1982) 'Accommodation of a scientific conception: Toward a theory of conceptual change', *Science Education*, **66**, 2, pp. 211–27.

RICHARDSON, V. (1994) 'Conducting Research on Practice,' *Educational Researcher*, **23**, 5, pp. 5–10.

SCHÖN, D.A. (1983) *The Reflective Practitioner: How Professionals Think in Action*, New York, Basic Books.

SCHÖN, D.A. (1987) *Educating the Reflective Practitioner*, San Francisco, Jossey-Bass.

SHULMAN, J.H. (ed.) (1992) *Case Methods in Teacher Education*, New York, Teachers College Press.

SHULMAN, J.H. and MESA-BAINS, A. (1993) *Diversity in the Classroom: A Casebook for Teachers and Teacher Educators*, Philadephia, Research for Better Schools, Hillsdale, NJ, Lawrence Erlbaum Associates.

STAKE, R. (1992) 'An evaluator's review of part 3 of the handbook 'The Curriculum as a Shaping Force', *Journal of Curriculum and Supervision*, **8**, 1, pp. 16–19.

VAN MANEN, M. (1991a) *The Tact of Teaching*, Albany, State University of New York Press.

VAN MANEN, M. (1991b) 'Reflectivity and the pedagogical moment: The normativity of pedagogical thinking and acting', *Journal of Curriculum Studies*, **23**, 6, pp. 507–36.

WHITE, R.T. (1988) *Learning Science*, London, Blackwell.

WHITE, R.T. and GUNSTONE, R.F. (1992) *Probing Understanding*, London, Falmer Press.

WHITEHEAD, J. (1993) *The Growth of Educational Knowledge: Collected Papers*, Bournemouth, Hyde Publications.

Author Index

Subject Index

Subject Index